ETHEREUM

DISTRIBUTED CONSENSUS

2013—2014—2015—2016—2017
A CONCISE ETHEREUM HISTORY BOOK

Ethereum—Distributed Consensus

by Christopher P. Thompson

Copyright © 2017 by Christopher P. Thompson

Book Author by Christopher P. Thompson

Book Design by C. Ellis

ISBN—13: 978-1546544821
ISBN—10: 1546544828

ETHEREUM

DISTRIBUTED CONSENSUS

2013—2014—2015—2016—2017
A CONCISE ETHEREUM HISTORY BOOK

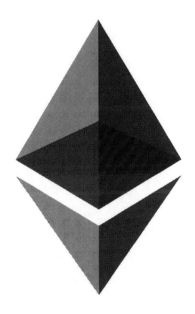

CHRISTOPHER P. THOMPSON

SPECIAL MENTIONS

Charles Ellis

Paul Thompson

Deborah Thompson

Kath Pannett

Chris Pannett

Julie Brooks

Shaun Brooks

CONTENTS

INTRODUCTION

Since the inception of Bitcoin in 2008, thousands of cryptocurrencies or decentralised blockchains have been launched. Most ventures into the crypto sphere have not gone to plan as their founders would have hoped. Nevertheless, there are currently hundreds of crypto related projects which are succeeding.

This book covers the history of Ethereum, an open-source, publicly distributed computing platform, from when the "Ethereum Whitepaper" was published in 2013 by Vitalik Buterin. It was not until the 26th January 2014 that the project was formally announced at the North American Bitcoin Conference. Since that time, development has been ongoing. Major topics covered in this book include:

- Initial publication of the Ethereum Whitepaper in 2013.

- Formal announcement at the North American Bitcoin Conference in 2014.

- Funds raised for development during the "Genesis Sale" in 2014.

- ÐΞVCON-0 took place in Berlin, Germany in 2014.

- Frontier was the first live release of the blockchain in the summer of 2015.

- ÐΞVCON1 took place at the Gibson Hall in London, UK in 2015.

- Homestead was the first production ready release and the first hard fork.

- The drama of The DAO occurred in the summer of 2016.

- ÐΞVCON2 took place at the Hyatt on the Bund in Shanghai, China.

- Two further hard forks to resolve the persistent DoS attacks in autumn 2016.

- Interest from institutional investors and global corporate enterprises.

- A market capitalisation surge in late winter 2016/17.

INTRODUCTION

To be specific, this book covers a concise chronological series of events from the 23rd January 2014 to the 17th March 2017. This is over three years of history. During this time, interest in Ethereum has grown from developers, speculators, banking, finance, insurance, software firms and cryptocurrency fanatics.

You may have bought this book because Ethereum is your favourite cryptographic blockchain. Alternatively, you may be keen to find out how it all began. I have presented the information henceforth without going into too much technical discussion about Ethereum. If you would like to investigate further, I recommend that you read material currently available online at the official website at https://www.ethereum.org/

If you choose to purchase a certain amount of Ether, please do not buy more than you can afford to lose.

Enjoy the book :D

WHAT IS ETHEREUM?

There are different definitions of Ethereum, unsurprisingly, which depend on how one perceives the technology. It is blockchain technology that goes beyond the sole purpose of currency. Some characteristics which help define it are:

- **Public blockchain**—anyone worldwide, who has the means and know-how, can access and participate in it.

- **Open-source** —development of the protocol is community driven. Input from developers, coders and programmers is possible.

- **Decentralised**—the network does not reside on a central server. Instead, the network is distributed over all computers which run the client software.

A commonly used definition of Ethereum is:

"A decentralized platform that runs smart contracts: applications that run exactly as programmed without any possibility of downtime, censorship, fraud or third party interference."

After an eighteen month research and development testing phase, the Ethereum blockchain went live on the 30th July 2015. Since then, there have been several upgrades to the underlying protocol code called hard forks. These were:

- Homestead kicked in on the 14th March 2016 (see chapter 7)

- The DAO hard fork kicked in on the 20th July 2016 (see chapter 8)

- Tangarine Whistle kicked in on the 18th October 2016 (see chapter 10

- Spurious Dragon kicked in on the 22nd November 2016 (see chapter 10)

One of the principal goals of Ethereum is to decentralise as much as possible using blockchain technology. Its developers have envisaged a new type of Internet.

WHAT IS ETHER?

It is the native cryptocurrency of the Ethereum ecosystem. In a similar manner to other cryptocurrencies such as Bitcoin, it can be traded on exchanges, sent or received between two entities or stored as an investment. It is listed under the diminutive ETH and has the symbol Ξ. Its prime purpose is to permit users to upload, execute and pay for ÐApps on the platform. It is also described as:

- The token value of the Ethereum Blockchain.

- The cryptofuel of the network protocol which makes the utilisation of decentralised applications (ÐApps) and smart contracts possible by users.

In July 2014, the following explained the necessity of Ether:

"Without the requirement of payment of Ether for every computational step

and storage operation within the system, infinite loops or excessive storage demands

could bog down Ethereum and effectively destroy it."

In order to distribute an initially unknown number of Ether, Ξ, to investors within an early community, a "Genesis Sale" occurred from the 22nd July 2014 to the 2nd September 2014. More information about the sale can be found on pages 39 to 41.

As is evident during the course of this book, the fiat value of one unit of Ether account can be very volatile. For example, when "The DAO" was hacked on the 17th June 2016, one Ether fell from approximately US$21 to US$13. Key dates on which its value surpassed certain US$ thresholds were:

Surpassed US$5 for the first time on the 11th February 2016
Surpassed US$10 for the first time on the 4th March 2016
Surpassed US$50 for the first time on the 17th March 2017

Interest from institutional investors spurred on the price of Ether to new heights.

SMART CONTRACTS

Smart contracts are computerised sets of rules, protocols or pre-determined agreements which govern how certain terms get executed. They can enforce the negotiation or performance of a contract between multiple parties. Several properties of these types of contract include:

- To minimise the need for trusted intermediaries.

- To mitigate the chances of fraud.

- To cut the costs of transaction or enforcement fees.

- To enforce a past agreement without the chance of dispute.

In effect, there is the potential for time to be saved by all parties. A cheaper, more secure and more reliable process is possible.

Nick Szabo, a computer scientist, was the first individual to use the phrase "smart contracts" back in 1994. In 1994, his definition was:

> **"A smart contract is a computerized transaction protocol that executes the terms of a contract. The general objectives are to satisfy common contractual conditions (such as payment terms, liens, confidentiality, and even enforcement), minimize exceptions both malicious and accidental, and minimize the need for trusted intermediaries. Related economic goals include lowering fraud loss, arbitrations and enforcement costs, and other transaction costs."**

One of the best known and reported smart contracts was "The DAO". It went live in late May 2016 and was subsequently exploited three weeks later. Other areas in which smart contracts could be applied include government, insurance, real estate, banking, supply chain, medicine and scientific research. Ultimately, smart contracts define the rules and penalties around an agreement in the same way that a traditional contract does, but also automatically enforces those obligations.

DECENTRALISED APPLICATIONS (ÐAPPS)

Often abbreviated ÐApps, they are pieces of software which operate from a global network of multiple computers. They are not downloaded or installed from one single central authority which has to be trusted by the user. They are described as more flexible, transparent and resilient than regular applications.

Over the past few years, developers have been busy designing, testing and launching an array of different ÐApps. Developers have been happy to present their innovative ÐApps at several conferences, events and meetups.

A website at http://dapps.ethercasts.com/ displays hundreds of ÐApps and their status. On the 1st May 2017, there were 398 recognised Ethereum ÐApps. Some examples of ÐApps currently available or being developed are:

- **Augur** —decentralised prediction market (Jack Peterson, Joey Krug)
- **Golem** —distributed computation (Piotr Zieliński)
- **FirstBlood.io** —decentralised eSports reward platform (Joe & Zack)
- **Swarm** —distributed file storage (Daniel Nagy)
- **Whisper** —group chat (Fabian Vogelsteller)
- **Ethlance** —decentralised job market platform (Matus Lestan)
- **Etherplay** —decentralised skilled games platform (wighawag)
- **Ether.Camp** —decentralised Ethereum block explorer (Roman Mandeleil)

ÐApps are likely to replace centralised applications over the coming years and decades. Facebook, Amazon, Google, and every other mainstream service being used on the Internet, function by using centralised systems. ÐApps are an emerging field with a lot of smart people experimenting with new models.

MILESTONE TIMELINE

14th December 2013 —Official Ethereum Reddit account founded

23rd January 2014 —Official Ethereum Bitcointalk thread created

26th January 2014 —Vitalik Buterin formally announced Ethereum at the North American Bitcoin Conference in Miami, FL, USA

29th January 2014 —Official Ethereum Facebook account founded

1st February 2014 —First PoC testnet clients released

7th February 2014 —First Ethereum AMA took place on Reddit

9th February 2014 —First Ethereum Go client went live on testnet

17th February 2014 —Second PoC testnet clients released

1st March 2014 —Third PoC testnet clients released

5th March 2014 —Ethereum team moved into the Swiss HQ in Zug

9th April 2014 —Fourth PoC testnet clients released

5th June 2014 —Vitalik Buterin awarded a Peter Thiel Fellowship

14th July 2014 —Ethereum Foundation was registered

22nd July 2014 —Fifth PoC testnet clients released

22nd July 2014 —The "Genesis Sale" began

8th August 2014 —Number of Ether pre-sold surpassed 50 million

2nd September 2014 —The "Genesis Sale" ended at 22:59 UTC

5th October 2014 —Sixth PoC testnet clients released

14th November 2014 —Vitalik Buterin received the World Technology Award for the most innovative software in 2014

24th November 2014 —First Ethereum Developer Conference, ÐΞVCON-0, began in Berlin, Germany

28th November 2014 —First Ethereum Developer Conference, ÐΞVCON-0, ended in Berlin, Germany

18th December 2014 —Jutta Steiner announced the "Bug Bounty Program"

MILESTONE TIMELINE

9th January 2015	—Community survey results unveiled
13th January 2015	—Seventh PoC testnet clients released
26th January 2015	—Bug Bounty Program began
24th February 2015	—Eighth PoC testnet clients released
28th February 2015	—New official Ethereum website went live
9th March 2015	—Subscribers of the official Ethereum Reddit surpassed 4,000 for the first time.
9th May 2015	—Ninth/last PoC testnet clients released
9th May 2015	—Olympic testing phase began
22nd July 2015	—Days remained until the launch of Frontier
27th July 2015	—Details on how to prepare for Froniter were released
30th July 2015	—Frontier launched at 15:26:13 UTC
30th July 2015	—Ming Chan selected as the Executive Director of the Ethereum Foundation
7th August 2015	—First Ethereum transaction took place on the live Frontier network
7th August 2015	—Ethereum was added to www.coinmarketcap.com
7th August 2015	—Gatecoin initiated live trading of Ether
7th August 2015	—Kraken initiated live trading of Ether
7th August 2015	—Coinsquare initiated live trading of Ether
8th August 2015	—Poloniex initiated live trading of Ether
11th August 2015	—ShapeShift initiated live trading of Ether
13th August 2015	—Cryptsy initiated live trading of Ether
14th August 2015	—Bittrex initiated live trading of Ether
15th August 2015	—Yunbi initiated live trading of Ether
20th August 2015	—Alcurex initiated live trading of Ether

MILESTONE TIMELINE

21st August 2015	—HitBTC initiated live trading of Ether
24th August 2015	—Cryptomate initiated live trading of Ether
26th August 2015	—Olympic testing rewards announced
3rd September 2015	—Stephan Tual amicably left the Ethereum Foundation
24th September 2015	—Venue of ÐΞVCON1 confirmed
1st October 2015	—Augur crowdsale completed
28th October 2015	—Microsoft announced as a sponsor of ÐΞVCON1
6th November 2015	—Tickets for ÐΞVCON1 had sold out
9th November 2015	—First day of ÐΞVCON1 at the Gibson Hall in London
13th November 2015	—Last day of ÐΞVCON1 at the Gibson Hall in London
23rd November 2015	—Bittylicious initiated live buys/sells of Ether
29th December 2015	—Livecoin initiated live trading on Ether
2nd January 2016	—C-Cex initiated live trading of Ether
11th January 2016	—Gavin Wood bid farewell to the core dev team
9th February 2016	—Ethereum became the second largest cryptographic blockchain in terms of market capitalisation
12th February 2016	—Ethereum market capitalisation surpassed US$500m
19th February 2016	—YoBit initiated live trading of Ether
22nd February 2016	—Exmo initiated live trading of Ether
29th February 2016	—Homestead client software was released
4th March 2016	—Fiat value per unit account of Ether surpassed US$10
7th March 2016	—Quoine initiated live trading of Ether
9th March 2016	—ETHEXIndia initiated live trading of Ether
11th March 2016	—QuadrigaCX initiated live trading of Ether
12th March 2016	—Ethereum market capitalisation surpassed US$1Bil
14th March 2016	—Bitfinex initiated live trading of Ether

MILESTONE TIMELINE

14th March 2016	—Homestead hard fork kicked in at 18:49:53 UTC
15th March 2016	—Bitcoin Indonesia initiated live trading of Ether
16th March 2016	—BTC Markets initiated live trading of Ether
22nd March 2016	—BX Thailand initiated live trading of Ether
23rd March 2016	—The Rock Trading initiated live trading of Ether
24th March 2016	—Vitalik Buterin gave a presentation at Coinbase
25th March 2016	—Korbit initiated live trading of Ether
29th March 2016	—Bitso initiated live trading of Ether
2nd April 2016	—BitBay initiated live trading of Ether
5th April 2016	—Venue of ÐƎVCON2 announced
11th April 2016	—Coinone initiated live trading of Ether
13th April 2016	—CEX.IO initiated live trading of Ether
14th April 2016	—bitFlyer initiated live trading of Ether
30th April 2016	—The DAO 28 day crowdsale began
9th May 2016	—Gemini initiated live trading of Ether
17th May 2016	—The DAO crowdsale became of largest in history
18th May 2016	—The DAO 28 day crowdsale ended
18th May 2016	—AlfaCashier initiated buy/sell of Ether
23rd May 2016	—Bter initiated live trading of Ether
24th May 2016	—GDAX initiated live trading of Ether
14th June 2016	—Microsoft announced as ÐƎVCON2 premiere sponsor
17th June 2016	—The DAO was exploited by way of code flaw
17th June 2016	—All time high market capitalisation of 2016 was attained at approx. US$1,739,839,634
21st June 2016	—Members of the Ethereum developer community launched a "whitehat" counter-attack on The DAO

MILESTONE TIMELINE

24th June 2016	—Soft fork fix to tackle DAO issues released
28th June 2016	—Soft fork vulnerability discovered
8th July 2016	—Official ÐƎVCON2 website went live
15th July 2016	—Hard fork software clients released
20th July 2016	—Second hard fork kicked in at 13:20:40 UTC
26th July 2016	—Vitalik Buterin addressed the subject of ETC
27th July 2016	—SpaceBTC launched the ETH/EUR trading pair
2nd August 2016	—Block number 2,000,000 was timestamped
22nd August 2016	—Santander announced as a ÐƎVCON2 sponsor
1st September 2016	—Dinar Dirham announced as a ÐƎVCON2 sponsor
3rd September 2016	—TuxExchange initiated the ETH/BTC trading pair
19th September 2016	—ÐƎVCON2 Ethereum Developer Conference began
21st September 2016	—ÐƎVCON2 Ethereum Developer Conference ended
26th September 2016	—FirstBlood crowdsale raised US$6,267,767
29th September 2016	—ICONOMI crowdsale raised US$10,682,516.42
13th October 2016	—third hard fork called Tangerine Whistle announced
13th October 2016	—a Ukraine-based called Liqui added Ether trading
18th October 2016	—third hard fork kicked in at block number 2,463,000
11th November 2016	—Golem crowdsale raised US$8,600,000
15th November 2016	—fourth hard fork called Spurious Dragon announced
22nd November 2016	—fourth hard fork kicked in at block number 2,675,000
30th November 2016	—Bitsane initiated ETH/BTC, ETH/USD and ETH/EUR
2nd December 2016	—an exchange called BTC Alpha added Ether
6th December 2016	—nine month low of one unit of Ether account
16th December 2016	—the database of the official Ethereum was compromised

MILESTONE TIMELINE

1st January 2017	—Market capitalisation was ~US$720,735,075
15th January 2017	—Block number 3,000,000 was timestamped
19th January 2017	—Collaboration began between Ethereum and Zcash
14th February 2017	—Vitalik released an update on Metropolis
28th February 2017	—The "Enterprise Ethereum Alliance" was launched
2nd March 2017	—eToro initiated live trading for Ether against USD
12th March 2017	—Market capitalisation surpassed US$2 billion
15th March 2017	—ÐƐVCON3 will take place in Cancun, Mexico
16th March 2017	—Market capitalisation surpassed US$4 billion
17th March 2017	—The value of one unit of Ether account surpassed US$50 for the first time

BLOCKCHAIN

Every cryptocurrency has a corresponding blockchain within its decentralised network protocol. Ethereum is no different in this sense. A blockchain is simply described as a general public ledger of all Ether transactions and blocks ever executed since the very first block, the Genesis Block. In addition it continuously updates in real time each time a new block is successfully mined, timestamped and verified. Blocks enter the blockchain in such a manner that each block contains the hash of the previous one. It is therefore utterly resistant to modification along the chain since each block is related to the prior one. Consequently, the problem of double-spending is solved.

After an eighteen month research, testing and development phase, the Ethereum blockchain was launched on the 30th July 2015. It was described as the first live release and was given the name Frontier (see chapter 5).

As a means for members of general public to view the blockchain, web developers have designed and implemented block explorers. They tend to present different layouts, statistics and charts. Some are more extensive in terms of the information given. Usual statistics included are:

- **Height of block** —the block number of the network.

- **Time of block** —the time at which the block was timestamped to the blockchain.

- **Transactions** —the number of transactions in that particular block.

- **Total Sent** —the total amount of cryptocurrency sent in that particular block.

- **Block Reward** —how many coins were generated in the block

  (added to the overall coin circulation).

PROOF OF WORK (PoW) MINING

Proof of work mining is a competitive computerised process which helps to maintain and secure the blockchain in such a way as to verify transactions and prevent double spending.

In the general sense of cryptocurrency, those who participate in the activity of mining are called miners. They are general members of the cryptocurrency community who dedicate processing power (hash) of their computers towards solving highly complex mathematical problems and verifying transactions. This process upholds the integrity and security of the network. As such, miners are described as protectors of the network. Each transaction (held within a certain block) is validated before adding it to the blockchain. By doing this, they are rewarded (as an incentive) with newly generated mined coins or transaction fees. These coins are issued by the software in a transparent and predictable way outside of the control of its founders and developers. A miner can be based anywhere in the world as long as they have an internet connection, sufficient knowledge of how one mines and the hardware/software required to do so.

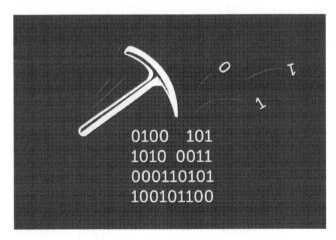

CRYPTOCURRENCY EXCHANGES

A cryptocurrency exchange is a site on which registered users can buy or sell Ethereum against BTC, USD and so on. Some exchanges require users to fully register by submitting certain documentation including proof of identity and address. On the other hand, most exchanges only require users to register with a simple username and password with the use of a currently held e-mail account.

Cryptocurrency exchanges across the globe have initiated Ether trading pairs on a regular basis. After Frontier was launched, there were several exchanges which immediately added Ethereum. Gatecoin, Kraken and Poloniex did not hesitate. Since then, other exchanges such as Bitfinex, GDAX, BTC-e and Gemini have gladly done the same.

Immediately below are the most popular exchanges in term of daily trading volume:

Exchange	Based
Poloniex	United States
Coinone	South Korea
GDAX	United States
Korbit	South Korea
Kraken	United States
Bitfinex	Hong Kong
Livecoin	United Kingdom
Yunbi	China
Gemini	United States
YoBit	Russia
Bittrex	United States
BTC-e	Russia

ETHEREUM COMMUNITY

A community is a social unit or network that shares common values and goals. It derives from the Old French word "comuntee". This, in turn, originates from "communitas" in Latin (communis; things held in common). Ethereum has a community consisting of an innumerable number of individuals who have the coin's well being and future goal at heart. Vitalik Buterin, Jeffrey Wilcke, Martin Becze, Péter Szilágyi, Dr. Christian Reitwiessner, Alex Van de Sande, Viktor Trón and Ming Chan are notable people.

At the time of publication, there are social media sites on which discussion and development of Ethereum take place. These are:

- **Facebook** -https://www.facebook.com/ethereumproject/

- **Official Forum** -https://forum.ethereum.org/

- **Reddit** -https://www.reddit.com/r/ethereum/

- **Twitter** -https://twitter.com/ethereumproject?lang=en

- **YouTube** -https://www.youtube.com/channel/ UCNOfzGXD_C9YMYmnefmPH0g

In essence, the community surrounding and participating in the development of Ethereum is the backbone of the coin. Without a following, the prospects of future adoption and utilisation are starkly limited. Ethereum belongs to all those who use it, not just to the founders who initially created it.

A CONCISE HISTORY OF ETHEREUM

I.   ETHEREUM WHITEPAPER PUBLISHED

II.   AGREEMENT THAT SOME SORT OF "GENESIS SALE" REQUIRED

III.   FOUR FIDUCIARY MEMBERS ANNOUNCED

IV.   AN INITIAL DEVELOPER TEAM ANNOUNCED

V.   PREPARATIONS MADE TO FORMALLY ANNOUNCE ETHEREUM

0

INITIAL HISTORY
OF ETHEREUM

"He is a co-creator and inventor of Ethereum, described as a "decentralised mining network and software development platform rolled into one" that facilitates the creation of new cryptocurrencies and programs that share a single blockchain (a cryptographic transaction ledger)." - Wikipedia description of Vitalik Buterin

As a consequence of the culmination of research and hard work, Vitalik Buterin published the original "Ethereum Whitepaper" on a cold November 2013 San Francisco day. This document describes a new type of blockchain in an innovative and technical manner. An objective had been put forward to improve upon the purpose of Bitcoin created and launched in January 2009. After frustrating amicable arguments between Bitcoin developers and himself, Vitalik Buterin, and the growing team besides him, wanted to create a peer-to-peer distributed blockchain which would allow its users to propose, design, test and execute any decentralised application (ĐApp) imaginable on top of it. Users would need Ether (the native cryptocurrency of the platform) in order to use it. In addition, a more robust scripting language for developing applications was sought after.

Over the following years, the road towards this goal would turn out to be challenging as well as rewarding. A new paradigm had begun.

Vitalik Buterin had been involved with Bitcoin since March 2011. His most well known project was Bitcoin Magazine which he co-founded with Mihai Alisie in September 2011. He made the decision to work on Bitcoin projects full time after he had left university in 2013.

Besides Vitalik, there were three other initial core members of the Ethereum team. They had all received a copy of the "Ethereum Whitepaper" and were intrigued by its content. Described by their corresponding roles at the time, they were known as fellow fiduciary members:

- **Charles Hoskinson**—Head of the Bitcoin Education Project.

- **Anthony DI Iorio**—Executive Director of the Bitcoin Alliance of Canada and founder of the Bitcoin Decentral coworkingspace in Toronto.

- **Mihai Alisie**—Founder and Chief Editor of Bitcoin Magazine.

They all agreed that some sort of "Genesis Sale" was required in order to fund future development and engage an initial community around the project. This would turn out to be very challenging over the first half of 2014 because of the innumerable regulations which had to be adhered to.

Some of the potential applications on the Ethereum platform were cited:

- User-issued cryptocurrencies or "coloured coins".

- Decentralised exchanges.

- Financial contracts (leverage, hedging etc.)

- Saving wallets with withdrawal limits.

- Gambling.

- Data storage.

- Personalised messaging.

Functionality of the C++ and Go implementations had reached a stage at which an official alpha testnet client was not far away. Marketing was also active with the aim of making the community as successful and efficient as possible. What follows is an list of other people who were involved with Ethereum at the beginning:

- **Dr. Gavin Wood**—Core C++ Developer.

- **Jeffrey Wilcke**—Lead Go Developer

- **Geff Obscura**—Core Go Developer.

- **Dr. Emanuele Costa**—Quantitative Analyst; SCRUM Master.

- **Joseph Lubin**—Software Engineering, Quantitative Analyst.

- **Eric Lombrozo**—Software Architect.

- **Max Kaye**—Developer.

- **Jonathan Mohan**—Media, Marketing and Evangelism (Bitcoin NYC).

- **Wendell Davis**—Strategic Partner and Branding (Hive Wallet).

- **Anthony Donofrio**—Logos, branding, Web development (Hive Wallet).

- **Taylor Gerring**—Web development.

- **Paul Snow**—Lanaguage development, software Development.

- **Chris Odom**—Strategic Partner, Developer (Open Transactions)

- **Jerry Liu and Bin Lu**—Chinese strategy and translations

- **Hai Nguyen**—Accounting

- **Amir Shetrit**—Business Development ("Colouted Coins").

- **Steve Dakh**—Developer (KryptoKit).

- **Kyle Kurbegovich**—Media (Cointalk).

They were looking forward to the "North American Bitcoin Conference" in Miami, FL, USA. Their focus was to bootstrap the vision established in the whitepaper. It was time to announce Ethereum to the wider cryptocurrency community. An official Ethereum Reddit account was created on the 14th December 2013.

I.   ETHEREUM FORMALLY ANNOUNCED IN MIAMI, FLORIDA, USA

II.   FIRST PROOF OF CONCEPT TESTNET CLIENTS RELEASED

III.   SWISS HQ OF ETHEREUM OPERATIONS ESTABLISHED

IV.   VITALIK BUTERIN AWARDED A PETER THIEL FELLOWSHIP

V.   ETHEREUM FOUNDATION REGISTERED ON THE 14TH JULY

1

ANNOUNCEMENT
OF ETHEREUM

"Derived from the latin "Aether", Aethereum is the "plural" of Aether. It means heaven, air or sky…"

Like almost all cryptocurrencies or cryptographic decentralised blockchains, an official Bitcointalk forum thread was created for Ethereum on the 23rd January 2014 at 11:33:17 UTC by user "Vitalik Buterin". It was originally titled "[ANN] Ethereum: Welcome to the Beginning". Nevertheless, development of the Ethereum Project had already begun. The wider Bitcoin community and beyond had become aware of a new promising and innovative project which wanted to expand on the original vision set out with Bitcoin. The initial core development team, and the other developers who had thereafter joined, wanted to shift blockchain technology to a new level.

Three days after the announcement on Bitcointalk, the core developers attended the "North American Bitcoin Conference" in Miami, Florida, USA. It was an event which had been scheduled for quite some time. Vitalik spoke on behalf of the team on stage for about thirty minutes in front of an intrigued audience of Bitcoin suppo-

-rters, developers, investors and other cryptocurrency fanatics. A video on YouTube is testimony to this event. He described Satoshi's objective to test two things simultaneously. These being:

- **Bitcoin the decentralised currency**—a money purely online that allows its users to send value anywhere in the world at low fees.

- **Bitcoin the blockchain**—a technology that is decentralised and trust free. It is a database one can add things to, but not remove things from.

He stressed the importance of these two being married together. The latter needs security which, in turn, requires an incentive for security (a currency with value). He also went on to describe some of the first applications on the blockchain besides currency. The first three of these he discussed were Namecoin (2010), Escrow Transactions (2011) and Coloured Coins (2012).

Ethereum received an incredible response after Vitalik had finished his speech. They were consequently overwhelmed with the unanticipated response from those who attended. It took hours for the developers to answer questions from interested and enthused parties.

After the conference, Gavin Wood (left the team in January 2016 to pursue other blockchain ventures) and Jeffrey Wilcke became full-time Ethereum developers. They had previously been working, respectively, on the C++ and Go clients on a part -time voluntary basis. At this time, Gavin, Jeffrey and Vitalik were the three initial primary core developers.

After listening to the community, the developers arrived at an initial preliminary funding model. They proposed a funding period beginning on the 1st February 2014 and ending at the end of the following month. It would consist of an initial issuance of 2,000 Ether per 1 BTC for the first seven days, 1,980 Ether on the eighth day, 1,960 Ether on the ninth day until a baseline of 1,000 Ether on the last three days. They promised that all Bitcoin raised would be centrally managed with high transparency and open accounting. The ultimate aim of the "Genesis Sale" would be to "breathe life" into an organisation as a means to optimise development, marketing and infrastructure. All details on how to access and participate in it were going to be published at http://funds.ethereum.org. They stressed the importance of only trusting official announcements. Any attempts from other sources to collect Bitcoin should be dismissed and reported.

There were understandably some people on the forums who did not trust the fiduciary members, but others sincerely said they were going to be "all in".

On the 29th January, after long discussions, the team decided to postpone the scheduled "Genesis Sale" until later notice. They required more time to create a proper infrastructure by reviewing all relevant regulations. They found themselves in unknown territory on the legality of what they were raising funds for. Charles Hoskinson was quoted as saying:

"As for the fundraiser, innovation requires fuel and thus we'll make sure we get to it as soon as we can as well. Our goal is to be as fair and equitable as possible."

As a consequence of work and travelling, the core developers had not had ample opportunity to answer the growing number of questions which they were receiving. Both Charles and Vitalik promised to participate in some sort of Q&A to address this later on. They valued the feedback they had already received.

On the 1st February, the expected release of the first proof of concept alpha testnet clients occurred. From this point, users could download, develop and test code. It would give users the opportunity to experiment with it before they decided to donate BTC towards the "Genesis Sale". They would also gain better understanding of what the Ethereum project is about before participating.

It brought Ethereum deserved growing attention from the cryptocurrency space.

During the month of February, there were several events which occurred:

- On the 4th February, a separate Bitcointalk forum thread titled "**** Official Ethereum QA thread ****" was created to allow questions to shift away from the official Ethereum thread on that forum.

- On the 7th February, the first Ethereum Reddit AMA (Ask Me Anything) took place. People were encouraged to ask Vitalik, Anthony, Charles and Mihai any questions they had. It happened from 18:00 EST and 21:00 EST.

- On the 9th February, the Go client went live on testnet.

- On the 11th February, Neal Koblitz, co-founder of elliptic curve cryptography, joined the Ethereum project as a Cryptography Advisor.

- On the 17th of February, the second PoC testnet clients were released.

- On the 19th February, the first smart contract went live on the testnet at 23:58 UTC. Namecoin was successfully implemented in nine lines of code.

On the 1st March, the developers were happy to release the third proof of concept (PoC3) clients on testnet. This was also the day on which an episode of the Keiser Report was broadcast including Charles Hoskinson as a guest.

Four days later, the team finally moved into the dubbed "Ethereum Spaceship" in the Canton of Zug in Switzerland. It became the Swiss HQ of Ethereum operations. Mihai Alisie had been scouting Switzerland over the past month in order to gain a clear legal strategy and financial business base for the project. He was pleased it had become reality. They viewed Switzerland as the centre of European finance and bastion of freedom of speech and human rights.

By the end of the month, some members of the community were growing restless for news about the upcoming "Genesis Sale". The development team wanted it to begin as soon as possible, but emphasised establishing a solid legal strategy beforehand. The exact structure of the "Genesis Sale" had not yet been finalised and had changed drastically since the first draft in January.

Announced on the 4th March, Bitcoin Expo 2014 took place from the 11th to the 13th April at the Metro Toronto Convention Centre in Canada. It was organised by the "Bitcoin Alliance of Canada". Prior to this, supporters of Ethereum were invited to meet the team in Toronto on the 9th April. Gavin Wood, Vitalik Buterin, Stephan Tual, Joseph Lubin and Jeffrey Wilcke were confirmed as attending, including others. The 9th April was also the day on which the fourth proof of concept (PoC4) testnet clients were released.

Over the last three months, the regulatory side of the project had been the main focus of attention. The Ethereum project had to abide by legal requirements in order to succeed. On the 20th May, the "Digital Finance Compliance Association" was established. Its prime purpose was to provide well intended guidance for the team to interact with the Swiss authorities.

On the 5th June, it was reported that Vitalik Buterin had been awarded a US$100,000 (paid over two years) Peter Thiel Fellowship alongside nineteen other people. It was viewed by the broader cryptocurrency community as recognition for the continuous effort and hard work he had been putting into Ethereum and other past and contemporary endeavours. PayPal co-founder and noted VC investor Peter Thiel emphasised the enthusiasm of such an award as it would help support innovators in their respective fields (financial support). He said:

"We hope the 2014 Thiel Fellows inspire people of all ages as they demonstrate that intellectual curiosity, grit and determination are more important than credentials for improving civilization."

Approximately one week later, Charles Hoskinson left the project. He had wanted Ethereum to form a venture capitalist-backed entity to develop the protocol and then use a non-profit organisation to launch a "Genesis Sale" afterwards. He disagreed with the road towards creating the Ethereum Foundation in Switzerland.

At the beginning of July, a global regulatory strategy had finally been established by the growing team. Preparations for the "Genesis Sale" were well underway. The system which would be used to administer the donations of Bitcoin was close to being set up. It was created by Taylor Gerring. Taylor Gerring posted details of how to proceed in purchasing Ether during the "Genesis Sale" on the official Ethereum website. It was a process which required an e-mail address and password.

On the technical side of the project, four different clients were in non-friendly user interface states, the mining/hashing algorithm had not yet been finalised (vision to make it CPU-friendly, and ASIC resistant) and the code was far from complete. The team encouraged developers of all hues to contribute to the open source code on GitHub.

On the 14th July, after the decision was made to adopt a non-profit organisation, the Ethereum Foundation (Stiftung Ethereum) was registered. Its purpose, amongst others, would be to manage the raised funds from the upcoming "Genesis Sale" in the best possible way. A dominating, but not exclusive, focus had been set on the promotion of the development of the Ethereum Protocol.

Members of the community were told to expect announcements from the foundation, technical, organisational or personal, on the official Ethereum Blog. These would also be linked to the official Facebook, Reddit and Twitter sites.

Shortly after the registration of the foundation, the "Genesis Sale" was announced. It would initiate a large network of developers, miners and investors. Financial backing for developers was sought after. They were going to pre-sell a software product called Ether, not a share in a company. The more Ether sold, the higher the initial number of Ether at launch. Ether would also allow users of the decentralised platform to upload, distribute, pay for, create and test ÐApps.

On the 22nd July, it was announced that the PoC5 testnet clients had been released. It was a significant release in the sense that, for the first time, both the C++ and Go clients began to effortlessly work together and process commands on the same blockchain. The developers had also managed to reduce the block time from sixty to twelve seconds.

Other events which occurred during this period of time were:

- On the 29th January, an official Facebook page was created at https://www.facebook.com/pg/ethereumproject/

- Gavin Wood published the Ethereum Yellow Paper that would serve as the technical specification for the Ethereum Virtual Machine (EVM).

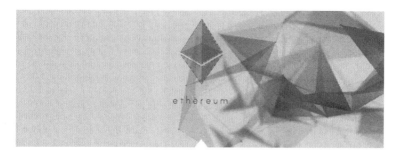

ether sale ends in:

9 : 9 : 28 : 35
Days Hours Minutes Seconds

Estimated ether purchased:

56,544,642 ETH

Current price:
1 bitcoin buys 1,430 ether

time remaining at current price:

0 : 9 : 28 : 35
Days Hours Minutes Seconds

next price: 1 bitcoin buys 1,400 ether

I.   GENESIS SALE BEGAN ON THE 22ND JULY 2014

II.   WITHDRAWALS FROM THE BTC DONATION ADDRESS BEGAN

III.   GENESIS SALE ENDED ON THE 2ND SEPTEMBER 2014

IV.   A TOTAL OF US$18,439,086 RAISED FOR DEVELOPMENT

V.   SIXTH PROOF OF CONCEPT TESTNET CLIENTS RELEASED

2

FUNDRAISING BEGAN

"In order to raise funds for development of Ethereum to the release of the genesis block and beyond, the Ethereum foundation conducted a sale of Ether to the public, during which anyone could buy Ether in exchange for Bitcoin at a rate of 1337 to 2000 ETH per BTC, with earlier purchasers getting better rates. The sale lasted 42 days, starting on July 22nd and ending at 23:59 Zug time September 2, and collected a total of 31,531 BTC, worth $18,439,086 at the time of the sale, in exchange for about 60,102,216 ETH."

After weeks of anticipation and deliberation, the "Genesis Sale" began on the 22nd July. It would last for forty two days. An initial issuance rate of 2,000 Ether per 1 BTC donated would exist for the first fourteen days. Investors who intended to go ahead with a purchase of Ether were advised to only trust information and updates on the official Ethereum website at https://www.ethereum.org/. This was also the place where all other relevant documentation would be posted. The Ethereum team encouraged the community to report all dubious and fraudulent material immediately.

There were a significant number of users on the forums who questioned what the total number of Ether available to purchase was, when they would receive their purchases and how the raised Bitcoin would be spent. There had been innumerable scams in the cryptocurrency space, so some users were unsurprisingly sceptical and were hungry for as much transparency as possible.

To be specific, the table immediately below shows the daily number of Ether promised to be given for each and every Bitcoin invested:

	Ether purchased per 1 BTC
Days 1-14 (22Jul to 04Aug)	2,000
Day 15	1,970
Day 16	1,940
Days 17-33	Number decreased by 30 each day
Day 34	1,400
Day 35	1,370
Days 36-42	1,337

As mentioned in the previous chapter, the prime purpose of the "Genesis Sale" was to create the necessary financial backing to pay for development of the project. A tentative launch date of the blockchain was scheduled for some time in the winter of 2014/2015. Everyone who participated in the sale would then be able to receive their Ether after that point in time. Ether, the "cryptofuel" of the Ethereum protocol, is not perceived as an ordinary cryptocurrency. It makes the utilisation of decentralised applications (ÐApps) possible by users. A quote at the time was:

"Without the requirement of payment of Ether for every computational step

and storage operation within the system, infinite loops or excessive storage demands

Within the first two hours of the "Genesis Sale", investors had purchased nearly 2.5 million Ether units of account. Slightly after twelve hours, this had increased to approximately 7.4 million. This equated to just over 3,700 BTC or ~US$2.3 million.

On the 25th July, a "Genesis Sale" FAQ was active for anyone who was having difficulties in how to proceed. Other advice and relevant facts were also accessible there. The team wanted to make sure no part of the community were left behind during this important phase of the project.

A total of just under US$6 million had been raised (taking the combined US$ values of each Bitcoin investment at the time of the transaction) by the end of July.

On the 8th August, it was reported that the number of Ether pre-sold had surpassed fifty million. As a consequence, the "Genesis Sale" had become the largest cryptographic token sale to date. A total of over 25,000 BTC had been raised. This equated to roughly US$14 million. This was also the day on which the Ethereum Foundation announced they would be withdrawing 4,150 BTC from the Exodus Address (fundraiser BTC wallet address). A further maximum of 850 BTC, if needed, was reserved for withdrawal before the end of the sale. These withdrawals would go towards paying for outstanding loans, compensating developer contributions and extending the number of team members. They released an "Intended Use of Revenue" chart and roadmap showing how the funds would be spent.

By the end of August, development had been accelerating quickly. Allocated funds for withdrawal from the Exodus Address had been used to expand operations.

On the 2nd September at 23:59 CET (zugtime) or 22:59 UTC, the "Genesis Sale" ended. By taking into consideration the US Dollar value of each and every BTC purchase, the final US Dollar value of each Ether unit of account was calculated at 0.306795. It had become the second highest crowdfunding project of all time (currently sixth). Figures compiled after the sale were:

- Development team raised a total of 31,531 BTC.

- Development team raised a total of US$18,439,086 US Dollars (multiplying each and every BTC transaction by the BTC US Dollar value at the time)

- Participants in the sale purchased a total of 60,102,216 ETH.

- There were a total of 9,007 ETH purchases.

Following on from the extremely successful "Genesis Sale", development of Ethereum continued to grow stronger. Development had recently been formalised under a non-profit organisation called Ethereum ÐΞV (a UK software firm under a non-profit-making agreement with the Ethereum Foundation). It operated from both London (the communications hub) and Berlin (ÐΞV hub). Vitalik Buterin, Gavin Wood and Jeffrey Wilcke were the initial directors of the organisation as well as being the original three core developers. It was no coincidence that these were the three people who designed and implemented the first functional clients. They were ultimately responsible for building and testing future software.

On the 5th October, the sixth experimental proof of concept clients were released. It was viewed as pivotal. Further reductions of the block time to six seconds had been stress tested. A newly developed GHOST-based protocol was utilised.

On the 26th October, the first Whisper-based ÐApp (the secure identity-based communications protocol) was released.

Also during the month of October, the Berlin hub became operational. Work began to hire talented individuals who would feel passionate about contributing towards and supporting the project. The core developers described this process as considerably more arduous than one may think, but worthwhile. Alex Leverington was the first person hired to work in Berlin. He had flown all the way from Texas to join the team. Before he joined on a permanent full-time basis, he had worked voluntarily since earlier in the year. His work focused on Mac builds.

Another notable person to accept the role of Office Manager of the ÐƎVHUB in Berlin was Christian Vömel. Christian had had many years experience including having worked in an international environment and had even taught office management. More hiring of people continued during November 2014.

Work in progress that is the Berlin Hub (ÐƎV hub)

In late October 2014, Gavin Wood and Jeffrey Wilcke decided to announce the first Ethereum Developer Conference to be held for a week in late November. It would be the responsibility of the UK software firm Ethereum ÐƎV to organise it. It was named ÐƎVCON-0.

On the 3rd November, a survey was initiated to last about two weeks. The team wanted to know if they were doing a great job at being transparent with the community. Described as a "community survey", its results would be published in early 2015.

On the 7th November, the Amsterdam hub became operational. A week earlier, they were in the clear to set it up after lawyers gave it the go ahead. Alex Van de Sande (aka avsa) was the first person to join the Amsterdam team. He was described as a gifted UX Engineer. The team were happy to have him onboard and admitted it was only a matter of time before he became an official member of the ÐΞV team.

As the first Ethereum Developer Conference drew near, further hiring had been taking place at the main hub operations in Berlin, Amsterdam and London. London had become the base of communications where at least four individuals had been hired to work on Mist (the Ethereum decentralised application browser). Berlin operations hub (established in Oct) focused on development of Whisper (Ethereum's P2P messaging system) and Swarm (Ethereum's client file distribution network). Stephan Tual, the former COO of Etherem, said much was happening behind the scenes and regular updates would be made about progress.

I.   VITALIK BUTERIN AWARDED THE WORLD TECHNOLOGY AWARD FOR THE MOST INNOVATIVE SOFTWARE IN 2014

II.   ÐƎVCON-0 BEGAN ON THE 24TH NOVEMBER IN GERMANY

III.   ÐƎVCON-0 WOULD LATER DRIVE FUTURE INITIATIVES

IV.   ÐƎVCON-0 ENDED ON THE 28TH NOVEMBER IN GRMANY

V.   JUTTA STEINER ANNOUNCED THE BUG BOUNTY PROGRAM

3

ETHEREUM ÐƎVCON-0 IN BERLIN

"In November 2014, ETH DEV organized the DEVCON-0 event, which brought together Ethereum developers from around the world to Berlin to meet and discuss a diverse range of Ethereum technology topics. Several of the presentations and sessions at DEVCON-0 would later drive important initiatives to make Ethereum more reliable, more secure, and more scalable."

Prior to the first ever Ethereum Developer Conference, a milestone event occurred at the 2014 World Technology Awards Summit at the "Time and Life Building" in New York City, USA. It occurred on the 13th-14th November. Vitalik Buterin had edged out Mark Zuckerburg (an American computer programmer and Internet entrepreneur) to receive the World Technology Award for the most innovative software in 2014. He was up against other nominees who included Jack/Laura Dangermond, Christian Lanng and Kira Radinsky. It was further official recognition and acknowledgement (inc. Thiel Fellowship in June) of his innovative work with Ethereum. Roger Ver, an early investor in Bitcoin, was quoted as saying:

"It is great to see members of the Bitcoin community getting the recognition they deserve from members of the IT community that are not directly involved with Blockchain technology. I think we will see more main stream recognition of the great minds involved with Bitcoin in the coming years."

On the 24th November, in the early hours of the morning, the first Ethereum Developer Conference called ÐƐVCON-0 kicked off. It was an opportunity for nearly all Ethereum developers to gather under one roof, meet face-to-face and share ideas. Over the five day period, there were successive presentations, discussions and workshops aimed at increasing everyone's knowledge, scope and direction of the project. What follows is a brief overview of the conference over that period.

On the first day, Gavin Wood gave a presentation titled "Welcome! Our mission: ÐApps". He began proceedings by thanking those people who had made the Berlin operation possible. He described how progress had led to the concentration of power. He set out a mission to decentralise this power. Everyone present had the opportunity to introduce themselves at the end of his talk. Other presentations on the day were made by Stephan Tual, Sven Ehlert and Alex Van de Sande.

On the second day, Gavin Wood and Christian Reitwiessner talked about the Solidity programming language; its vision and the roadmap ahead in order to fully complete it. Four other speakers on this day were Marek Kotewicz, Piotr Zielinski, Sven Ehlert and Lefteris Karapetsas. It was a day primarily focused on programming languages and ÐApps.

On the third day, Vinay Gupta led a workshop during which time attendees were asked to describe Ethereum in 30 seconds. There was diverse opinion in the room. Two other speakers called Martin Becze and Jeffrey Wilcke spoke about their clients. A panel discussion consisting of Gavin Wood (Ethereum C++), Jeff Wilcke (Ethereum Go), Heiko Hees (Pythereum) and Martin Becze (Node-Ethereum) ended the day. They took it in turns to talk about the characteristics of their clients.

On the fourth day, discussions focused on the security and robustness of the network. Sven Ehlert, Jutta Steiner and Heiko Hees held a workshop based on stress testing. A presentation followed by Christoph Jenzsch who went through the different developer tests and tools available. Jutta Steiner also spoke about future security audits of the network from external bodies and a soon to be initiated bounty campaign to reward those who tested the network. Ultimately, a stable release of the Genesis block was being worked towards. Three other presentations by Alex Leverington, Gavin Wood and Daniel Nagy capped off the day.

On the final day, Vitalik Buterin, who was joined by Vlad Zamfir later on, talked about the scalability (the network's potential to handle ever growing traffic) of Ethereum. They both described the importance of light client protocols which would allow clients to run on low capacity devices such as mobile phones and tablets. Other presentations by Juan Batiz-Renet and Gavin Wood followed. Gavin Wood talked about Mix. Vitalik closed the day after going through ideas pertaining to Ethereum 2.0 (the next stage of development).

Specific presentations at the conference would later drive important initiatives in the project to make it more reliable, secure and scalable. Ultimately, it helped developers consolidate knowledge to prepare for the highly awaited launch next year. All attendees were thanked for making the event possible.

On the 18th December, Jutta Steiner, who was responsible for the security audit of the code before the launch of Ethereum, announced an upcoming "bug bounty program" for those who wanted to get rewarded for testing the network.

Developer interest in Ethereum had grown steadily throughout 2014. Frequent posts on the official Ethereum blog had kept the community informed of progress and the road ahead. In addition, the official forum and Reddit websites were attracting an ever growing, enthusiastic and motivated community.

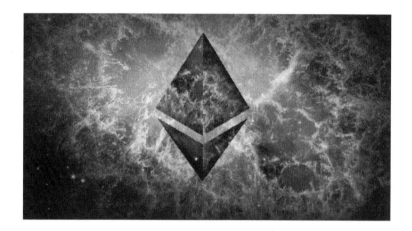

I.   RESULTS OF A COMMUNITY SURVEY UNVEILED

II.   BUG BOUNTY PROGRAM BEGAN

III.   INCENTIVISED OLYMPIC TESTING PERIOD KICKED OFF

IV.   PROJECT DESCRIBED AS SECURITY, NOT SCHEDULE DRIVEN

V.   PREPARATIONS MADE BEFORE THE RELEASE OF FRONTIER

4

PROGRESS TOWARDS
THE GENESIS BLOCK

"Working through all issues will take the time it takes. It's a security-driven not schedule-driven process, after all." - Jutta Steiner

A new year brought with it renewed prospects for Ethereum on both the technical and community sides. Core developers Vitalik Buterin, Gavin Wood and Jeffrey Wilcke kept the community up-to-date on progress. By February, there were plans underway to reform the foundation by turning it into a professional entity.

Other areas of high priority were:

- The release strategy (steps to be taken towards the Genesis Block).

- The bug bounty program (officially began on the 26th January 2015).

- The formation of partnerships with third parties in the crypto space.

On the 9th January, the results of the survey initiated in November were published. Its purpose was to guide the project forward by engaging with the broader community. There were a total of 286 submitted responses to 14 questions.

Question one was "Which country do you currently reside in?". Answer:

123 (43%) in North America, 114 (40%) in Europe, 30 (10%) in Asia,
13 (5%) in Oceana and 6 (2%) in South America.

Half of the questions posed required the surveyee to answer either Strongly Disagree (1), Disagree (2), Neither Disagree Nor Agree (3), Agree (4) or Strongly Agree (5). These were as follows:

	1	2	3	4	5
ETH is transparent with its community?	3.5 %	8.4%	14.7%	46.9%	26.6%
ETH is transparent with its finances?	3.8%	11.2%	31.5%	37.4%	16.1%
ETH is spending its funds wisely?	2.1%	7.0%	48.6%	35.3%	7.0%
ETH's use cases in society are clear?	5.9%	12.9%	18.9%	40.2%	22.0%
ETH is progressing from a software perspective?	2.4%	6.3%	19.9%	46.2%	25.2%
ETH's mission statement is clear?	2.4%	7.0%	48.6%	35.3%	7.0%
You understand how ETH works technologically?	1.9%	9.9%	17.5%	52.4%	18.4%

An important question, "Of the following aspects, do you think we should be focusing more or less or about the same on them?", was posed. At the top of the list to be focused on the most were the client user interfaces (UI). Other aspects to focus more on were "ease of installation" and "client reliability". The answer to this question helped the team gain a better perspective on what had be worked on the most before the launch of the blockchain. Two aspects of least importance were "social media" and "implementation of client languages".

Other information gained from the survey:

- Over 66% of respondents thought a mobile client was important to them or their business, because it would increase the usability of Ethereum.

- Over 50% chose either Alethzero (CPP) or Pythereum (Python) as the Ethereum clients they were using.

- 42% chose Linux was their favourite OS development environment.

- 51% chose Serpent (Python) as their preferred programming language.

50

Alex Van de Sande was thanked for his help with the survey implementation and chart graphics.

As had been the case since the first proof of concept testnet releases on the 1st February 2014, there were two further releases in the first two months of 2015:

- PoC7—13th of January 2015

- PoC8—24th of February 2015

At the very beginning of March, it was announced that Vinay Gupta had been installed as the release co-ordinator of Ethereum. He joined the Ethereum team at the end of 2014 to manage the security audits. It was his job to help make sure of a productive, smooth and step-by-step strategy towards the first release of the Genesis Block. It had already been stated that the team were not going to rush the release, but rather make sure things got implemented correctly and were functionally optimised to iron out bugs/code flaws. No date of release had been finalised (project not schedule driven, but security driven). Some of the ways in which the community could stay up-to-date with progress were highlighted. All tools and expertise would be used to create a great and promising decentralised ecosystem.

Four phases in the release process were planned to happen throughout the coming years. Each one would add new features and improve upon the user friendliness, robustness and security of the platform. These being:

1. **Frontier**—to initiate the live blockchain (not testnet) in bare command-line format. An interface to allow mining and execute smart contracts for pros.

2. **Homestead**—similar to Frontier with further protocol upgrades. It would move away from beta phase Frontier, but still was command-line driven.

3. **Metropolis**—will be the official release with a full-featured user interface for non-technical users. Mist will also launch alongside a ÐApp Store. Further improvements are planned.

4. **Serenity**—a shift from the current proof of work timestamping algorithm will occur. An innovative proof of stake algorithm is being researched.

On the 9th May, the ninth and final release in the proof of concept testnet series happened. It signalled the last phase of development before the first live release of the Ethereum blockchain. It was given the name Olympic. Its main purpose was to reward people who were willing to test the network to its limit.   This was accomplished via an incentivised usage of the testnet after which testers would be able to claim their reward from a total prize fund of 25,000 Ether. Prizes included:

- A grand prize of at least 5,000 for the person or miner who successfully created a substantial hard fork between the Go and C++ clients. This fork had be on the main chain; one client must accept the block with the other client rejecting it.

- Four other categories offered a top prize of 2,500 Ether plus smaller prizes. These included categories such as transaction activity, virtual machine usage, mining prowess and general punishment.

Vitalik Buterin, Gavin Wood and Jeffrey Wilcke would judge each category and all prize-winners would be entitled to have their name immortalised in the Ethereum Genesis block. To be considered for a prize, users had to send an e-mail to olympic@ethereum.org. Suffice it to say, those in the employ of Ethereum or its subsidiaries were not eligible.

It was time to test the network's resilience, robustness and readiness.

At the beginning of July, Vinay Gupta updated the community on the security of the Ethereum network and all corresponding clients. The security audit began at the end of 2014. Its prime purpose was to ensure maximum security before the launch of the blockchain. He was pleased to have seen very high quality submissions to the bug bounty program. It had helped enormously in the development process. There were still funds left in the allocated budget for further submissions (the bug bounty program was still operational at the time). Vinay Gupta was quoted as saying:

"As we draw closer to release, security and reliability is increasingly uppermost in our minds, particularly given the handful of critical issues found in the Olympic test release. We are very grateful for the enthusiasm and thorough work that all auditors have done so far."

On the 22nd July, Stephan Tual notified the community that only days remained until the launch of Frontier. He expected eager engagement from early adopters and application developers who would initiate the live Ethereum ecosystem. At this moment, Frontier was described as "feature complete" and the team were reviewing the final steps. There was no set launch time and no centrally launched blockchain. It would emerge from technical consensus.

Users were also made aware of an initial "thawing period". It would prevent transactions for the first few days, but would allow miners to begin their operations and early adopters to install their clients without rushing. A mandatory small software update (for all clients) would end this period.

On the 27th July, all useful details on how to prepare and what to expect were made public on the official website and associated blog. Any users who needed further guidance were advised to get help via the official forums or chatrooms.

Other events which occurred in this period were:

- On the 28th February, a new revamped official Ethereum website went live.

- On the 9th March, the number of subscribers to the official Ethereum Reddit page (www.reddit.com/r/ethereum) surpassed 4,000.

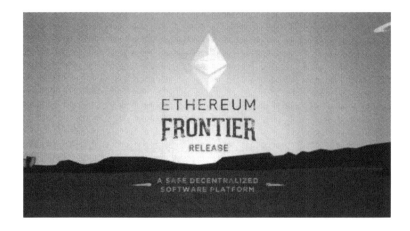

I.   ETHEREUM BLOCKCHAIN WENT LIVE ON 30TH JULY 2015

II.   ELEVEN EXCHANGES INITIATED ETHER TRADING

III.   FINANCES OF THE FOUNDATION DISCLOSED

IV.   AUGUR CROWDSALE ENDED

V.   MICROSOFT ANNOUNCED SPONSORSHIP OF ÐΞVCON1

5

ETHEREUM BLOCKCHAIN LAUNCHED (FRONTIER)

"A few minutes ago, many of you generated and loaded the Ethereum Genesis Block, marking the inception of Frontier, the first Live release of the Ethereum Project." - Stephan Tual

More than one year and a half after Vitalik Buterin published the first version of the "Ethereum Whitepaper", the blockchain finally launched on the 30th July 2015 at 15:26:13 UTC. Approximately 72 million Ether were contained in the Genesis Block. Users were now able to mine, not trade or transact, the platform's native token, Ether (ETH, Ξ). Frontier was an initial barebones, command line implementation specifically designed and intended for use by developers as a live testing environment. It was the result of months of work by hundreds of talented and professional people. Despite this, regular users were still able to download and install the client software, but were reminded of the associated risks. If one lacked the knowledge or skill, they were encouraged to wait for a more user friendly future release. Vinay Gupta was quoted as saying:

"Don't put a lot of value at risk unless you really, really are sure you know what you are doing, and you're confident about your risk assessment of the network."

Members of the Ethereum Foundation expected early adopters, miners and application developers to begin utilisation of the live ecosystem straight away. As mentioned in the previous chapter, users would not be able to send and receive Ether until the "thawing period" had ended.

Block #0 (Reward 5 ETH) July 30th 2015 at 03:26:13 PM UTC

Another event on the 30th July was the result of a new organisational structure at the Ethereum Foundation. After an intensive recruitment process, Ming Chan (1) was selected as the Executive Director of the foundation. Three other individuals were also selected to join the Board of Directors besides Vitalik Buterin (the President of the Board). That is to say, Lars Klawitter (2), Wayne Hennessy-Barrett (3) and Dr. Vadim David Levitin (4) were on board. This structure was deemed necessary before the team could focus on the next step of development.

| 1 | 2 | 3 | 4 | 5 |

On the 31st July, a cryptocurrency exchange called Poloniex, familiar to anyone who regularly trades cryptocurrencies, announced they would make Ether trading available as soon as the "thawing period" was over.

As promised before the launch of the blockchain, at least three centralised exchanges were ready to initiate trades of Ether. These three were Gatecoin, Kraken and Poloniex. On the 6th August, users of Kraken were able to place buy orders for Ether with BTC and other supported fiat currencies (ETH/EUR, ETH/USD, ETH/CAD, ETH/GBP, or ETH/JPY).

On the 7th August, as soon as trading activity on exchanges had begun, a website, which ranks cryptocurrencies according to market capitalisation, trading volume and gain/loss called www.coinmarketcap.com, added Ethereum. The first known market capitalisation was recorded at US$193,464,826. This was also the day on which the very first Ether transaction occurred (the thawing period had ended).

Eleven known cryptocurrency exchanges initiated Ether trading during August:

	Trading Initiated	Trading Pairs	STATUS
Gatecoin	7th August 2015	BTC, EUR	ACTIVE
Kraken	7th August 2015	BTC, USD, EUR, GBP, REP, CAD, ICN, ETC	ACTIVE
Coinsquare	7th August 2015	BTC	ACTIVE
Poloniex	8th August 2015	BTC, USD, ETC, REP, ZEC, GNT, ETC, LSK	ACTIVE
Shapeshift	11th August 2015		ACTIVE
Cryptsy	13th August 2015		CLOSED
Bittrex	14th August 2015	BTC, ETC, DGD	ACTIVE
Yunbi	15th August 2015	CNY	ACTIVE
Alcurex	20th August 2015	BTC	ACTIVE
HitBTC	21st August 2015	BTC, EUR	ACTIVE
Cryptomate	24th August 2015	GBP	CLOSED

Historically the first exchange to add trading of Ether, Gatecoin is licenced and based in Hong Kong, China. It was founded in July 2013 by former investment banking professionals including CEO Aurélien Menant.

Kraken opened, after a long beta testing phase, on the 10th September 2013. BTC, LTC and EUR were initially available for trading. Kraken was established on the 28th July 2011. Jesse Powell is the CEO and a co-founder.

The third exchange to initiate trades of Ether on the 7th August was Canadian based Coinsquare. On the 11th November 2014, Coinsquare went live with ten trading markets including BTC, LTC and DOGE.

Poloniex was established on the 19th January 2014. It is based in the United States. It is by far the highest ETH/BTC volume trading market. Over 160 BTC trading pairs and 14 USD trading pairs are active on their platform.

ShapeShift, a Swiss based web platform, was founded in 2013. Erik Voorhees is the founder and CEO. They made it possible for their customers, who do not require to register an account with them, to buy/sell Ether on the 11th August.

On the 13th August, Cryptsy initiated Ether trading against Bitcoin. Two days later, it added ETH/USD as well. It was an exchange based in Delray Beach, FL, USA. It launched on the 20th May 2013. However, it no longer exists.

Bittrex is based and fully regulated in the USA. It allowed its users to begin trades of Ether against Bitcoin on the 14th August.

Yunbi, formerly known as Peatio Exchange, was founded in July 2013. After a nine month trial period, they went live on the 1st April 2014. They are based in China. It became possible to trade Ether on Yunbi on the 15th August.

Alcurex initiated the trading pair ETH/BTC on their exchange on the 20th August.

On the 21st August, HitBTC announced that Ether was available to trade against Bitcoin. Launched on the 14th February 2014, it is an exchange based in Europe. It went on to initiate its second Ether trading pair (ETH/EUR) on the 6th August 2016.

On the 24th August, CryptoMate allowed users to buy Ether on their exchange via instant bank transfer.

CRYPTOMATE

On the 26th August, the Ethereum Foundation announced the rewards of the Olympic testing period. UK software firm Ethereum ÐΞV thanked everyone who participated in it. It helped to determine the limits of the Ethereum ecosystem before Frontier was released. The top miner received 2,500 ETH for mining 57,744 blocks and the top sender received 2,500 ETH for sending 5,429,042 transactions. Other equivalent or smaller rewards were also given out.

On the 2nd September, George Hallam (External Relations at the Ethereum Foundation) had disappointing news regarding the upcoming ÐΞVCON1 event in London, UK. It had been indefinitely postponed after attempts to secure a venue for the dates 5th-8th October 2015 had fallen through. It would not be until the 24th of September 2015 that a new venue and time came to light.

Stephan Tual   **George Hallam**

On the following day, Stephan Tual broke the news that he had decided to leave the team on mutual terms. He cited personal circumstances for his departure and vowed to keep promoting the Ethereum ecosystem.

Over the next couple of weeks, the foundation were in the phase of restructuring their communication activities. Members of the London communications team were leaving or reducing their involvement. It was ample opportunity to reassess how the foundation were interacting with the community.

On the 28th September, Vitalik Buterin said he was proud of how far Ethereum had progressed. It had grown substantially on a global scale. Major financial institutions, software giants, governments, corporations and other small businesses had shown interest and subsequently investigated how they thought it could best suit their needs. Over one hundred decentralised applications had been designed, tested and executed so far.

Despite the successes, there were still ongoing challenges. These were technical, organisational and social. One aspect was the realisation that most work had been done by the foundation and its subsidiaries. It was expected that the wider community would take an increasing role (become the primary driver) in the success of Ethereum with the foundation in the lead role.

Also on the 28th September, details were disclosed of the Ethereum Foundation's finances. It had become publicly known, after the Bitcoin fiat price had decreased since the 2nd September 2014, an approximate US$9 million funding shortfall was the case. A hiring schedule that was meant to last over three years was now projected to last a little under two years. They reported their current financial holdings as roughly US$2.52 million (200,000 CHF*, 1,800 BTC and 2,700,000 ETH).

They also disclosed a 490,000 CHF* legal defence fund (aka insurance) and their approximate monthly expenditure of ~410,000 CHF*. Other means to raise money for future development included workshops, conference tickets, sponsorships, donations and tutorial courses.

Another challenge which faced the foundation was that the project had changed substantially since the beginning. It had grown from being a simple attempt to improve upon Mastercoin, by adding a programming language, to a sophisticated effort to push forward a powerful and expansive vision of a "Decentralised Internet". Vitalik Buterin was quoted as saying:

"To make it as easy to build secure, globally accessible and trust-minimized decentralized applications as it is to build a website – and hopefully even easier."

Vitalik Buterin was undeniably convinced that the foundation and its subsidiaries alone did not have the manpower to push the entirety of the vision through to its ultimate completion. Everyone was welcome to make Ethereum successful.

At the end of September, the market capitalisation of Ethereum was approximately just above US$53 million. It had gradually been decreasing throughout the month of September:

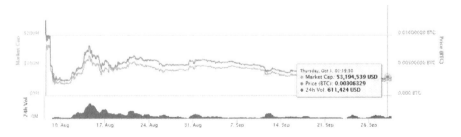

*CHF is the currency and legal tender of Switzerland and Liechtenstein

On the 1st October, news broke that Augur had raised roughly US$5,133,000 via a forty five day crowdsale in order to support future development. In doing so, it became one of the top twenty five highest crowdfunding projects of all time. It is a decentralized prediction market platform that aims to better explore the concept of "wisdom of crowds" and try to get more accurate predictions about future events. Development of Augur began in autumn 2014.

On the 22nd October, the Ethereum Foundation announced Nick Szabo as the keynote speaker of ÐΞVCON1. His keynote would focus on the history of the blockchain and smart contracts. Vitalik Buterin was quoted as saying:

"We are thrilled to welcome Nick to DΞVCON1. His pioneering work on smart contracts and the evolution of blockchain technology will add a tremendously valuable perspective to the conference."

Another ÐΞVCON1 related news story occurred six days later. Microsoft confirmed that they would sponsor and attend the event. Vitalik Buterin said he was very excited to work with Microsoft. Marley Gray, a spokesperson for Microsoft who was driving blockchain strategy there, was quoted as saying:

"We find the Ethereum blockchain incredibly powerful and look forward to collaborating within the Ethereum Community. We see a future where the combination of Microsoft Azure and Ethereum can enable new innovative platforms like Blockchain-as-a-Service. This will serve as an inflection point to bring blockchain technology to enterprise clientele."

This was also the day on which Microsoft introduced a toolkit which allows its users to build on the Ethereum protocol. To be more specific, users of Microsoft's cloud-based Azure service could access Ethereum "Blockchain as a Service".

Over the next couple of weeks, the Ethereum Foundation and ΞTHÐΞV were very busy organising and preparing for ÐΞVCON1 in London, UK. Vitalik Buterin described it as an event which would show supporters, developers, investors and the wider cryptocurrency community how large the ecosystem had become.

I.   TICKETS FOR ÐƎVCON1 HAD SOLD OUT

II.   ÐƎVCON1 BEGAN ON THE 9TH NOVEMBER 2015

III.   BITTYLICIOUS INITIATED BUYS/SELLS OF ETHER

IV.   LIVECOIN INITIATED LIVE TRADING OF ETHER

V.   ETHEREUM OVERTOOK RIPPLE IN TERMS OF MARKET CAP

6

ETHEREUM ĐƐVCON1

"Application developers are seeing that the Ethereum platform is a very powerful technology that offers advantages in a very broad set of areas. There has been a lot of interest in Ethereum applications over the last few months; particularly in January the number of individuals and companies interested in Ethereum private chains, Ethereum-based financial applications, smart contracts, IoT, etc, has all increased greatly." - Viltalik Buterin

On a grander scale than the first Ethereum Developer Conference held the previous year, the Ethereum Foundation, its subsidiaries and the wider community had been preparing to showcase how far the project had grown since inception. Hundreds of developers, entrepreneurs, business leaders and cryptocurrency enthusiasts were expected to attend the five day event called ĐƐVCON1 at the Gibson Hall in London, UK. Nick Szabo, Vitalik Buterin, Marley Gray, Don Tapscott and others were scheduled speakers. Ethereum had now become as recognisable as, and on par with, Bitcoin. Confirmed sponsors of the event included Microsoft, Slock.it and ConsenSys (a blockchain software technology company founded by Joseph Lubin).

Three days before the conference began, tickets had sold out. There had been a special 20% discount price for anyone who paid with Ether. It was also known prior to the 9th November that the event would be live streamed on YouTube. The audience was truly global.

On the first day of ÐƎVCON1, the 9th November 2015, the topics of discussion were about the ongoing research into Ethereum, the distributed platform. Ming Chan, the Executive Director of the Ethereum Foundation, opened proceedings by introducing Viltalk Buterin, Jeffrey Wilcke, Alex van de Sande and Gavin Wood. They spoke in this order and each individually described their role and how they were working to drive the project forward. Other presentations on first day were:

- Vitalik presented "Scalable Blockchains & Asynchronous Programming".

- Vlad Zamfir talked about the future proof of stake (Casper) Serenity release.

In the morning, there was a panel discussion consisting of Vitalik Buterin, Vlad Zamfir, Gavin Wood, Martin Becze and Dominic Williams. They discussed several strategies on the subject of scalability.

On the second and third days of the conference, discussion was primarily dedicated to the tools and methods being used to build robust, successful and effective decentralised applications (ÐApps). Developers admitted that there were many practical challenges to overcome to achieve optimum reliability, security and ultimate user experience. Alex Van de Sande, Christian Reitwiessner and Fabian Vogelstellar presented technical material pertaining to building ÐApps.

Three major speeches during these two days were given by:

1. Marley Gray—Microsoft Announcing Ethereum Blockchain as a Service.

2. Don Tapscott—How Blockchain Technology Can Help us Achieve Prosperity.

3. Vitalik Buterin—Understanding the Ethereum Blockchain Protocol.

Other presentations and panel discussions demonstrated how far development had progressed and matured. In particular, ways in which the protocol could be utilised were covered. Gavin Wood talked about the decentralised application called Whisper (Ethereum's peer-to-peer messaging system).

On the penultimate day, the conversation shifted to the myriad of ÐApps being developed or already available. Dr. Jack Peterson was the first speaker (9:00am UTC) who enthusiastically spoke about Augur, the decentralised prediction market platform. Other ÐApps being built using the Ethereum blockchain were also discussed on the 12th November 2015:

- **Maker**—is a decentralized autonomous organization on the Ethereum blockchain seeking to minimize the price volatility of its own stable token — the Dai — against the IMF's international currency basket SDR.

- **Gnosis**—is based on Ethereum. It is described as the next generation blockchain network. Its users are able to speculate on anything with an easy -to-use prediction market.

- **Colony**—makes it easier for people all over the world to build companies together online.

- **Ujo Music**—is a home for artists that allows them to own and control their creative content and be paid directly for sharing their musical talents with the world.

- **Backfeed**—development of governance schemes and economic models for Decentralized Organizations, enabling a true collaborative economy using blockchain technologies.

- Other decentralised applications presented at the conference covered areas such as synthetic assets, registries, batch auctions and a decentralised Reddit.

On the final day, Nick Szabo opened proceedings with a presentation titled "History of the Blockchain". He talked about previous attempts to create secure digital currencies. He considered Ethereum to be a great opportunity to secure value in a decentralised manner. Other speeches that morning were made by Taylor Gerring ("Ethereum in the Enterprise Environment"), Joseph Lubin ("Towards a Dynamic Economic, Social and Political Mesh") and Gavin Wood ("Ethereum for Dummies").

Slightly after noon UTC, a panel consisting of Vinay Gupta, William Mougayar, Joseph Lubin and Gavin Wood had a conversation about several strategies which could be used to increase the adoption of Ethereum. Integration of the brand into already familiar technology such as web browsers was suggested. A speech by William Mougayar titled "Communicating the Ethereum Narrative" followed.

Presentations based on the theme of social implications of Ethereum took place during the afternoon. Energy, banking, insurance, reputation systems, supply chain traceability and legal perspectives were topics of discussion.

In closing, Vinay Gupta took to the stage to present "Dangerous Old Men: Cypherpunk's Failure, Ethereum's Success". He repeatedly emphasised the importance of Ethereum being financially sustainable. This would go a long way towards guaranteeing continued support for research, development, infrastructure and attracting the best innovative minds in the field. Otherwise, the project would become rotted, hollowed out and irrelevant. He did not, as he thought others concurred, want to repeat the failures of past crypto movement endeavours.

Straight after Vinay, the closing words of Vitalik Buterin on the fifth day were:

"The Ethereum community has grown. It's attracted people from all parts of the world, and one of my favorite parts about this space is the sheer diversity, the quality, the different kinds of people that we've attracted. This isn't just about a currency and this isn't just about even one particular platform. This is a movement. It's a movement of software developers, of mathematicians, of political activists, entrepreneurs, social entrepreneurs, banking executives, and I think this week we've seen just about everyone represented. The community to me is probably my favorite part of this whole thing. So thank you all, and I hope to see you next year."

The last day appealed to industry, investors, policy makers and mainstream audiences, specifically people from outside the Ethereum community who wanted to understand how the project could best suit their interests. More than four hundred attendees forged better connections within the community and gained better understanding and knowledge of the future direction of Ethereum.

BITTYLICIOUS

On the 23rd November, Bittylicious made it possible to purchase Ether on their platform by using either GBP or EUR. After five days of beta testing, the platform went live on the 24th June 2013. They had provided a service to anyone with a UK bank account to quickly purchase Bitcoins. Marc Warne founded Bittylicious.

During December, videos of ÐΞVCON1 were being regularly uploaded to YouTube. Updates on Ethereum were very slim. Nevertheless, research and development was still ongoing behind the scenes. December was obviously a time for family and friends.

On the 29th December, an exchange called Livecoin integrated the trading pair ETH/BTC. They became operational on the 15th April 2015 after a testing phase. Two other trading pairs, ETH/USD and ETH/RUR, became operational on the 7th June 2016.

As the world welcomed 2016, Ethereum was getting closer to Homestead. Efforts continued to drastically cut the development and administrative costs of the project. In order to shift towards a more robust foundation, measures taken were:

- A number of ETH-based companies had taken the burden off the foundation.

- An increased transparency of the research and development process.

- They actively welcomed feedback on the best ways to improve upon social media, documentation and tutorials.

- Out of six entities across Europe in 2015, three had been decommissioned or were heading towards being shutdown. A smaller location in Zug had been established, the London location had shutdown and the foundation was looking at whether or not to cut rental costs in Berlin.

On the 2nd January, C-Cex initiated live trading of Ether against BTC and USD.

C-CEX.com @CryptoCurEncyX 2 Jan 2016
CCᴱˣ #Ethereum integrated! Industry fastest
Deposits / Withdrawals at your service!
c-cex.com/?p=eth-btc
c-cex.com/?p=eth-usd
#exchange

On the 7th January, it was reported that the Ethereum Foundation's monthly expenditures had been reduced from just over 400K EUR to about 175K EUR. Assets of the foundation of roughly 2,250,000 ETH, 500 BTC and US$100K were disclosed. Assuming that both the Ether price and their budgeting preferences remained unchanged, they projected it would keep them going for about one year.

On the 9th February, the market capitalisation of Ethereum (the total fiat price of all Ether unit of accounts mined to date) overtook that of Ripple to become the second largest. Market capitalisations according to www.coinmarketcap.com were:

	8th February 2016	9th February 2016
Bitcoin, BTC	US$ 5,750,430,888	US$ 5,698,163,225
Ethereum, ETH	US$ 238,447,790	US$ 279,709,312
Ripple, XRP	US$ 273,582,410	US$ 264,355,383

A renowned individual in the crypto sphere called Erik Voorhees, CEO of ShapeShift.io, announced (see below left) that Ethereum (ETH, Ξ) had just superseded Ripple (XRP) to acquire second place behind Bitcoin (BTC):

Erik Voorhees
@ErikVoorhees
⚏ Follow

Ethereum overtakes Ripple for #2 spot by market cap, up 13% today on $14mm volume CoinCap.io #bitcoin #cryptocurrency

On the 19th February, YoBit initiated three trading pairs of Ether against BTC, USD and RUR. It is a cryptocurrency exchange platform founded in Russia on the 5th January 2015. YoBit's ETH/BTC pair is in the top 10 in terms of volume.

Over the next few months, the foundation were confident of further cost savings, but wanted to increase the expenditure on the research and development of Serenity. Before they felt comfortable looking for ways to raise further capital, they were insistent on being more efficient with what they already had.   During February, Vitalik Buterin was quoted as saying:

"The first reason is that people have come to trust that the network is solid and reliable. Ethereum has had eight months of live network to prove just that. Secondly, users have noticed that the network is being constantly improved with new products and new services, which is a major attraction for new users who eventually buy ether and consequently push up the price."

Other events which occurred during this period were:

- On the 11th January, Gavin Wood published an official Ethereum blog article in which he said farewell to the core development team.

- One unit of Ether account went above US$5 for the first time ever on 11th February 2016.

- On the 12th February, the market capitalisation surpassed US$500 million.

- On the 22nd February, Exmo initiated the ETH/BTC trading pair.

Block #1,000,000 (Reward 5 ETH) February 13th 2016 at 10:54:13 PM UTC

I. SECOND MAJOR VERSION CALLED HOMESTEAD RELEASED

II. MARKET CAPITALISATION SURPASSED US$1 BILLION

III. EXCHANGE BITFINEX INITIATED TRADES OF ETHER

IV. BLOCK NUMBER 1,150,000 TIMESTAMPED

V. ETHEREUM FOUNDATION ANNOUNCED ÐΞVCON2

7

HOMESTEAD:

FIRST HARD FORK

"Homestead's arrival will begin to demonstrate the next generation of blockchain technology, whereby anything we can dream of, can be accomplished in a decentralised manner using Ethereum" - Andrew keys (co-founder of ConsenSys Enterprise)

On the 29th February, the second major version release (first production ready release) of Ethereum called Homestead was made available. It was described as more stable and secure (moved away from beta Frontier). It included many protocol improvements which users had to upgrade to in order to be on the correct chain. It would permit further network upgrades. A hard fork at block number 1,150,000 was announced and scheduled to happen on Pi Day. The developers were now happy to remove the scratched out word "safe" from the official website. Homestead marked a move to a more user friendly interface.

On the 4th March, the price of each and every Ether unit of account surpassed US$10 for the first time on both the Poloniex and Kraken ETH/USD trading markets. This was further recognition of the growing number of users, supporters and investors. Interest continued to escalate from major financial institutions, cryptocurrency exchanges, software firms and so on.

Since the beginning of the year, the market capitalisation of Ethereum had been climbing to new record highs on a regular basis. It increased from approximately US$70 million on the 1st January to just over US$500 million on the 12th February. Exactly one month later, on the 12th March, the market capitalisation surpassed US$1 billion (~1/6 that of BTC) for the first time ever. What follows are the Bitcoin values of one unit of Ether account (1 ETH) on the 12th March. They were the top nine exchanges in terms of Ether trading volume. In addition, the statistical website www.cryptocompare.com was used to source these figures:

	Price	Low	Open	Close	High	Volume
Poloniex	0.029675	0.02620	0.02674	0.03261	0.03353	2,332,438.19
Kraken	0.029625	0.02620	0.02675	0.03250	0.03298	746,376.98
Gatecoin	0.029685	0.02630	0.02676	0.03261	0.03300	196,959.07
Bittrex	0.029595	0.02639	0.02650	0.03269	0.03293	79,946.92
Exmo	0.029690	0.02629	0.02703	0.03235	0.03300	5,616.41
Yunbi	0.030750	0.02650	0.02710	0.03440	0.03440	2,558.66
Quoine	0.029500	0.02700	0.02700	0.03200	0.03200	1,631.07
HitBTC	0.030575	0.02586	0.02693	0.03422	0.03450	1,999.70
C-Cex	0.029615	0.02590	0.02590	0.03333	0.03500	528.44

It is plain to see that Poloniex and Kraken were, in terms of daily Ether trading volume, the dominant exchanges. These markets are still active today.

There was immense enthusiasm within the community that Ethereum was gaining huge recognition. Several months of solid development had given investors confidence that Ethereum had a promising future ahead.

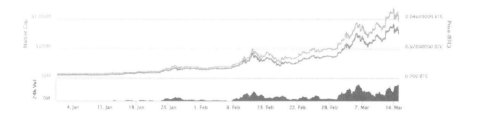

On the 14th March at noon UTC, Ether live trading began on the exchange called Bitfinex. Deposits of Ether into Bitinfex had been possible two days prior to this. Both trading pairs ETH/BTC and ETH/USD had been initiated.

Bitfiniex is a Hong Kong based exchange founded in 2012.

BITFINEX

Customer requests to add the option to trade Ether besides cryptocurrencies such as Bitcoin and Litecoin had been sky high. In addition, trading volumes of Ether at other exchanges had become "hard to ignore" by the Bitfinex team. In the first 24 hours of trading, Bitfinex had an approximate 25% share of the total ETH/USD market (see chart on right below). They were second only to Kraken (Poloniex were third). In terms of ETH/BTC, the top exchanges, in descending order of volume, were Poloniex, Kraken, Gatecoin and Bitfinex. As shown in the chart below (left), the ETH/BTC trading pair was the dominant pair over all known exchanges:

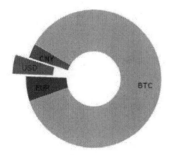 

On the same day at 18:49:53 UTC, block number 1,150,000 was timestamped. The developers and wider community celebrated this event on a live Google Hangout session as the software smoothly implemented the protocol changes. There were expectations of an increase in the number of decentralised applications (ÐApps) being developed, tested and uploaded such as prediction markets, music platforms and asset trading systems.

Block #1,150,000 (Reward 5 ETH) March 14th 2016 at 06:49:53 PM UTC

Throughout the month of March, ten additional exchanges initiated trading of Ether against other units of account. These were:

- On the 7th March, Quoine initiated live Ether trading against all ten supported fiat currencies on its platform. Two days later, the pair ETH/BTC launched. Mike Kayamori is the CEO.

- On the 9th March, ETHEXIndia initiated the trading pair ETH/INR.

- On the 11th March, a Canadian exchange called QuadrigaCX initiated both ETH/BTC and ETH/CAD. They have offices based in Vancouver, BC.

- On the 15th March, Bitcoin Indonesia initiated the trading pair ETH/BTC.

- On the 16th March, an Australian based exchange called BTC Markets opened both ETH/BTC and ETH/AUD for live trading.

- On the 18th March, ETH/USD and ETH/RUB went live on Exmo. ETH/BTC was already an option.

- On the 22nd March, BX Thailand made it possible for their customers to trade Ether (ETH) against both Bitcoin (BTC) and the Thai Baht (THB).

- On the 23rd March, an exchange called The Rock Trading (based in Malta) initiated the trading pairs ETH/BTC and ETH/EUR.

- On the 25th March, a South Korean exchange called Korbit initiated the trading pair ETH/KRW.

- On the 29th March, a local exchange in Mexico called Bitso was proud to initiate ETH/MXN.

On the 2nd April, the Polish cryptocurrency exchange called BitBay initiated the trading pairs ETH/BTC, ETH/USD, ETH/EUR and ETH/PLN. They were the first exchange to offer Bitcoin trading in Poland in 2014. Justyna Laskowska, a member of the BitBay team, said the indicators for Ethereum looked great going forward.

Three days later, the Ethereum Foundation and Wanxiang Blockchain Labs jointly announced they had combined two events into one. Both ÐΞVCON2 and the 2nd Global Blockchain Summit would occur from the 19th to the 24th September 2016 at the same venue. It would be held at the Hyatt on the Bund in Shanghai, China. Both events the preceding year were sold out venues.

Since Homestead kicked in, an increasing number of Bitcoin businesses had begun to investigate Ethereum. They wanted to know if it would benefit their operations. Uphold, BTCS and Ledger had already announced ETH initiatives. There had been curiosity and hesitancy over whether Ethereum would gain traction or not. Interest in adoption/utilisation had grown significantly after a number of key technical milestone goals were achieved.

Other events which occurred during this period were:

- Number of subscriber on www.reddit.com/r/ethereum surpassed 10,000 for the first time.

- On the 24th March, Vitalik Buterin gave a presentation at the headquarters of San Francisco BTC Startup Coinbase.

- On the 30th March, the Solidity programming language became available to use on Microsoft's Visual Studio.

- On 30th March, DigixDAO Crowdsale ended. The sale concluded in 12 hours as the maximum was reached and surpassed. A total of US$5.5 million was raised. It was the first gold standard token on the Ethereum platform. It Was also described as the first major "Distributed Autonomous Organisation" on the platform.

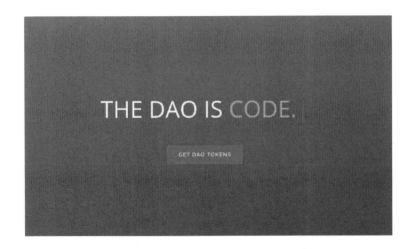

I. THE DAO CROWDSALE RAISED ABOUT US$160 MILLION

II. BTC-E, GEMINI AND GDAX INITIATED ETHER TRADING

III. THE DAO WAS HACKED/EXPLOITED

IV. ALL TIME HIGH MARKET CAP OF 2016 ATTAINED

V. A DECISION TO HARD FORK THE BLOCKCHAIN WAS MADE

8

THE DAO AND ALL TIME HIGH 2016 MARKET CAPITALISATION

""We actually don't know who started it. Of course we can see the address on the blockchain but we don't know who owns the address. The only way to speak with the DAO is to make a proposal and vote." - Christoph Jentzsch (co-founder of slock.it)

During April 2016, a registered company in Germany called Slock.it were proud to announce The DAO (a Decentralised Autonomous Organisation). They viewed is as a true representation of the ideals of decentralisation. Instantiated by the Ethereum blockchain, it was intended as a hub to support Ethereum related projects. It was ultimately meant to be a stateless (no physical address), leaderless (nobody in formal managerial roles) and open-source business model of smart contracts. Instead of one individual or group, it would be at the discretion of the DAO token holders who would decide where invested funds would be directed to. They would use their voting power to help determine which projects got funded. There would also be the possibility of participants receiving dividends in return for supporting certain projects. The DAO was described as being completely transparent; everything is done by the code, which anyone can see and audit. The DAO was owned by everyone who purchased DAO tokens.

Over the following few months, questions were asked about the exact origin of The DAO. Developers at Slock.it had built upon open-source GitHub software which had resulted from a complex network of relationships. The computer code behind the organization was written by Christoph Jentzsch, and released publicly on GitHub. Simon Jentzsch, Christoph Jentzsch's brother, was also involved in the project.

On the 28th April, a long standing exchange called BTC-e initiated Ether trading against both BTC and USD. It was founded in July 2011 and is based in Russia. Other trading pairs went live during 2016. These were ETH/LTC on the 1st May, ETH/RUR on the 30th May and ETH/EUR on the 29th September.

BTC℮

On the 30th April, the 28-day sale of DAO tokens began. A corresponding official website went live at http://daohub.org. Funding milestones were as follows:

- Raised more than US$50 million worth of Ether by the 12th May 2016.

- Raised more than US$100 million worth of Ether by the 15th May 2016.

- It became the highest crowdfunding campaign ever on the 17th May 2016.

- Raised more than US$150 million worth of Ether by the 21st May 2016.

On the 28th May, the crowdsale ended. A total of approximately US$160 million (the value of the sale end of 11.58 million Ether raised) had been raised by 18,000+ investors. The funds amounted to ~14.4% of all Ether in circulation. It still remains the largest crowdfunding campaign in history. Cryptocurrency exchanges immediately began to support the trading of DAO tokens. Since its inception, The DAO had inspired both passionate supporters and dire sceptics.

Two days later, three individuals, Dino Mark, Vlad Zamfir and Emin Gun Sirer, called for a moratorium on proposals. A white paper had been published which analysed the problems in The DAO's design and offered solutions to fix the flaws. These flaws could potentially encourage participants to act strategically rather than honestly.

As had been the case in each prior month of 2016, cryptocurrency exchanges were still initiating Ether trading. Gemini was the first to do so in May. They were thrilled to announce support for Ether on an official blog post on the 5th May. Two trading pairs ETH/BTC and ETH/USD were subsequently initiated on the 9th May at 9:30 AM EDT. Cameron Winklevoss, co-founder and President at Gemini, said:

"Our approval makes Gemini the first licensed ether exchange in the world. It also makes the NYSDFS the first regulatory agency in the world to supervise ether, reaffirming their position as the leading financial regulator in the area of digital assets."

It opened up for trading Bitcoin on the 8th October 2015 after they had received approval to launch from the New York State Department of Financial Services (NYSDFS).

Another major exchange called Coinbase initiated trading of Ether against both Bitcoin and USD on the 24th May. This coincided with the exchange being rebranded to GDAX (Global Digital Asset Exchange). On their official blog, they were quoted as saying:

"We believe Ethereum marks an inflection point for the industry. Ethereum's advanced scripting language enables new developments such as self-executing contracts, decentralized funding models, and autonomous governance structures."

On the 9th June, Peter Vessenes publicly disclosed the existence of a critical security vulnerability overlooked in the codebase of The DAO. Three days later, Stephan Tual said no DAO funds were at risk due to the vulnerability.

Fives days later, the Ethereum Foundation were pleased to announce Microsoft as the Premiere Sponsor of the upcoming ÐΞVCON2 conference. Vitalik Buterin said:

"We are very happy to have Microsoft's sponsorship for Devcon2 and highly appreciate their continued support and collaboration with the Ethereum Foundation and the Ethereum ecosystem. We look forward to continuing to work together in the future."

During the morning of the 17th June, The DAO was hacked/code flaw exploited by an individual or group. Ether was slowly being drained from it with the balance falling below 9 million Ether from 11.58 million raised. In total, 3.6 million Ether (~US$60 million) of funds originally committed to The DAO were transferred to a separate "Child DAO" by the attacker. News initially broke on Reddit and other social media platforms. Vitalik Buterin posted the following on Reddit:

"<DAO ATTACK> Exchanges please pause ETH and DAO trading, deposits and withdraws until further notice. More info will be forthcoming ASAP."

Griff Green, a spokesperson for Slock.it, also announced what was happening:

"The DAO is being attacked. It has been going on for 3-4 hours, it is draining ETH at a rapid rate. This is not a drill."

Fortunately, something called the "splitting mechanism" gave developers about 27 more days for a solution to be found to recovers the funds (put into account subject to a 28 day holding period under the terms of the Ethereum contract). The attacker would not be able to spend/withdraw the stolen Ether until the 15th July. In order to prevent further drains of Ether and retrieve the funds, the foundation and community developers initially proposed to implement a soft fork (no rollback of blockchain). The Ethereum blockchain was described as perfectly safe. Miners were advised to carry on as normal and DAO token holders advised to remain calm).

Straight after the incident, there was a contested debate about how to proceed. The DAO had already been highly discussed. There were a few options to take:

- Implement a hard fork which would rollback the blockchain.

- Implement a soft fork which would prevent the attacker from accessing, or at least prevent their movement, the Ether after the holding period.

- Do absolutely nothing.

Stephan Tual, COO of Slock.it, said The DAO was definitely going to close. The project's success or failure could have implications for the overall confidence in its underlying technology, Ethereum.

This was also the day on which the 2016 all time high market capitalisation of Ethereum was attained. It equated to roughly US$1,739,839,634 according to the website www.coinmarketcap.com. An average Bitcoin Satoshi value across all exchanges of 2,780,420 was also evident on that site. A historical chart from the site shows the ascent of both these values from 01/01/2016 to 17/06/2016:

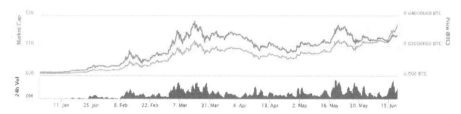

There had been a substantial increase from US$70 million at the beginning of 2016. At the all time high, the market capitalisation of Ethereum had increased 24 fold.

What follows is a table of ETH/USD values across the top five exchanges in terms of daily Ether trading volumes on the 17th June:

	Price	Low	Open	Close	High	Volume
Bitinfex	18.24	11.51	20.86	15.61	21.69	1,348,726.99
Kraken	18.14	13.51	20.74	15.54	21.49	520,476.36
BTC-e	17.28	12.82	19.56	14.99	20.50	150,189.48
Poloniex	18.00	13.00	20.50	15.50	21.40	135,834.30
GDAX	18.42	13.75	21.09	15.75	22.00	122,187.18

To coincide with the prior ETH/USD values, the ETH/BTC values were:

	Price	Low	Open	Close	High	Volume
Poloniex	0.023945	0.01722	0.02695	0.02094	0.02799	4,610,108.63
Kraken	0.024245	0.01640	0.02699	0.02150	0.02800	1,775,086.81
Bitfinex	0.023945	0.01770	0.02692	0.02097	0.02810	1,288,879.68
BTC-e	0.024440	0.01770	0.02796	0.02092	0.02796	212,262.93
GDAX	0.024005	0.01713	0.02693	0.02108	0.02826	142,517.78

All figures tabulated above were sourced from www.cryptocompare.com.

Four days later on the 21st June, members of the Ethereum developer community launched a "Whitehat" counter-attack on The DAO using a similar exploit the attacker used. Alex Van de Sande tweeted the following:

"DAO IS BEING SECURELY DRAINED. DO NOT PANIC"

This happened slightly after word had emerged on social media that more funds were being siphoned from associated contracts of "The DAO". During the evening of the 21st June, another tweet was posted by Alex Van de Sande:

"DAO is now mostly empty. 7.2M ether have been secured so far. The community needs to help by identifying the rest."

Work was ongoing to recover the stolen Ether and eventually draw a line under the drama of "The DAO". Uncertainty caused by how the situation would be resolved and how the resolution may be received from all quarters had been making the value of Ether on exchanges fluctuate wildly. Historical figures of ETH/USD from Bitfinex from the 18th June to the 23rd June were:

	Price	Low	Open	Close	High	Volume
18th June	13.30	10.13	15.19	11.41	15.30	869,090.63
19th June	11.50	10.55	10.76	12.43	13.36	326,846.06
20th June	12.12	10.51	12.33	11.90	12.49	317,579.64
21st June	12.31	11.20	11.67	12.94	12.98	184,202.19
22nd June	13.50	12.95	13.75	13.25	15.90	522,625.86
23rd June	13.51	12.50	13.26	13.73	14.00	149,030.43

On the 24th June, the Ethereum Foundation released a "Soft Fork" client. Its objective was to place a hold on funds siphoned from The DAO. Mining pools voted to enable it. It was not long until a new vulnerability was found with this approach on the 28th June. A tweet was posted by Fabian Vogelsteller, a lead application developer at the Ethereum Foundation, who said:

"With the soft fork being vulnerable there are two options left: a hardfork only affecting The DAOs, or doing nothing."

From the 28th June to the 15th July, there were many days of intense arguments in the Ethereum community about the pros and cons of implementing a hard fork. Critics of a hard fork argued would go against the immutability of blockchain technology. Other critics pointed to the fact it would bail out failure.

On the 8th July, the official ÐΞVCON2 website went live. More updates were planned to be announced there as the event drew near. This was also the day on which the Ethereum community unanimously voted in favour of a hard fork. Developers were already working hard on the code. They knew it was vital to make sure things were done properly during this pivotal time.

On the 15th July, a hard fork was announced. Exchanges, miners and developers were notified of a new specification. Christoph Jentzsch was quoted as saying:

"All DAO tokens, whether in white or dark DAO, child or main DAO, innocent or not innocent split, will be frozen and sent to a new contract address where DAO token holders will be able to withdraw their share."

A final decision was made to hard fork the Ethereum blockchain at block number 1,920,000. Miners overwhelmingly began to support the hard fork over the following days.

Other events which occurred during this period were:

- On the 11th April, Coinone exchange initiated ETH/KRW trading pair.

- On the 13th April, CEX.IO added both ETH/BTC and ETH/USD. On the 3rd June, they also initiated the trading pair ETH/EUR. Project developement of the exchange started in January 2013. Ten months later in November 2013, the company CEX.IO LTD was registered.

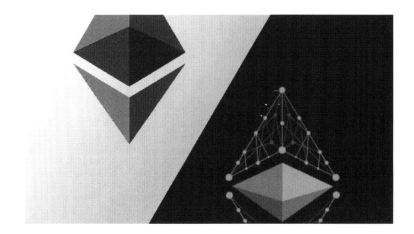

I. SECOND HARD FORK OCCURRED ON THE 20TH JULY 2016

II. VITALIK ADDRESSED THE SUBJECT OF ETHEREUM CLASSIC

III. BLOCK NUMBER 2,000,000 WAS TIMESTAMPED

IV. SANTANDER ANNOUNCED AS A GOLD SPONSOR OF ÐΞVCON2

V. DINAR DIRHAM ANNOUNCED AS A PLATINUM SPONSOR OF ÐΞVCON2

9

ETHEREUM HARD FORK CREATES TWO BLOCKCHAINS

"What I witnessed during this time was remarkable feedback and support from many different sides. A lot of work needed to be done, and many people came literally out of nowhere and helped in many ways." - Christoph Jentzsch

After weeks of uncertainly, controversy and cautious decision making, the Ethereum blockchain hard forked. On the 20th July at 13:20:40 UTC, block number 1,920,000 was timestamped to the blockchain by the China based Ethereum miner BW.com. It successfully and smoothly executed an "irregular state change" which transferred all Ether from the "Dark DAO" and "Whitehat DAO" contracts into the "WithdrawDAO Recovery" contract. Approximately 85% of miners mined the forked chain. With immediate effect, original DAO token holders were receiving their Ether back.

Many were surprised that miners continued to mine blocks and trade the original chain. A separate blockchain called Ethereum Classic, ETC was born.

Block #1,920,000 (Reward 5 ETH) July 20th 2016 at 01:20:40 PM UTC

On the 21st July, the market capitalisation of Ethereum once again surpassed US$1 billion for the fifth time. It had been below this value since the 1st July. Ether still remained one of the top cryptocurrencies on the market. Derived from the top three exchanges in terms of ETH/USD Ether trading volumes, fiat US Dollar currency prices of one unit of Ether account on the 21st of July were:

	Price	Low	Open	Close	High	Volume
Bitfinex	12.54	12.03	12.52	12.55	12.75	152,784.88
GDAX	12.71	12.10	12.58	12.84	13.09	71,786.16
Kraken	12.58	12.03	12.59	12.57	12.91	56,068.66

On the 26th July, Vitalik Buterin addressed the subject of Ethereum Classic and its implications for the core Ethereum community moving forward. He said the Ethereum Foundation would support the blockchain which included a hard fork meant to enable investors to recover funds lost in the collapse of The DAO. There was uncertainty whether both ETH and ETC would be supported. They did not wish to hinder the alternative classic chain. Vitalik Buterin was quoted as saying:

"We recognize that the ethereum code can be used to instantiate other blockchains with the same consensus rules, including testnets, consortium and private chains, clones and spin-offs, and have never been opposed to such instantiations."

Buterin sought to help technical users get on their desired chain. Responses to his statement were understandably divided on the philosophical lines of Ethereum Classic being described as the fork which best represents the values of the project. Over the last two days, the market capitalisation of ETC had increased 260% from US$66 million to US$162 million.   A number of users were still dissatisfied with the decision the Ethereum developers took to hard fork.

At the end of July, the market capitalisations of Ethereum and Ethereum Classic were approximately US$980 million and US$150 million respectively.

On the 2nd August, the 2,000,000th block was mined and timestamped to the Ethereum blockchain:

Block #2,000,000 (Reward 5 ETH) August 2nd 2016 at 09:32:58 PM UTC

On the 22nd August, it was reported that 2.29 million Ether (~US$25.9 million) out of the total retrieved ~11.6 million Ether were still remaining in the "WithdrawalDAO" account. Former investors had been able to withdraw their Ether straight away after the hard fork on the 20th July. It only took a matter of hours for nearly half the funds to be repatriated. After two days, nearly 60%. Matthew Tan, founder of ethereum block explorer Etherscan, was quoted as saying:

"Those who knew how to do it or wanted to withdraw [have] already done so."

On the 25th August, Santander were announced as a gold sponsor of the upcoming ÐΞVCON2. They have about 200,000 employees worldwide and have expanded heavily since the turn of the century. Many subsidiaries, such as Abbey National, were rebranded under the Santander name. According to George Hallam, External Relations at the Ethereum Foundation, the event was nearly sold out.

Other events which occurred during this period were:

- On the 27th July, an exchange called SpaceBTC launched the trading pair ETH/EUR. They are an European trading platform headquartered in London and founded on 20th November 2015.

- On the 1st Sept,ember Dinar Dirham, a decentralized gold trading platform, were announced as a Platinum Sponsor of DEVCON2.

- On the 3rd September, an exchange called TuxExchange opened ETH/BTC pair for live trading.

I.   ÐƎVCON2 BEGAN ON THE 19TH SEPTEMBER 2016

II.   MICROSOFT WERE THE PREMIERE SPONSOR OF ÐƎVCON2

III.   THIRD HARD FORK CALLED TANGERINE WHISTLE OCCURRED

IV.   FOURTH HARD FORK CALLED SPURIOUS DRAGON OCCURRED

V.   VALUE OF ONE ETHER DESCENDED TO A NINE MONTH LOW

10

ETHEREUM ÐƐVCON2 AND TWO MORE HARD FORKS

"The most important Ethereum presentation event of the year, developers from all over the world will join together to present their projects, ideas and 'proof-of-concepts'. The conference is the second installment of the original DEVCON —which was held in London, 2015."

As the highly anticipated event called ÐƐVCON2 approached, the market capitalisation of Ethereum had been slowly rising. According to www.coinmarketcap.com, it had risen from ~US$956,973,546 on the 8th September to ~US$1,077,726,264 on the 18th September (12.6% increase). Similar to ÐƐVCON1, numerous speeches, panel discussions and presentations were scheduled to be made by developers and other registered speakers.

As part of Shanghai International Blockchain Week, ÐƐVCON2 kicked off at 01:00 UTC (9:00 Shanghai Time) on the 19th September. Ming Chan opened proceedings with a 2-3 minute introductory talk during which time she appreciated the generosity of the event sponsors (they were on display as a billboard on stage) and smaller community sponsors. Major sponsors were Microsoft (Premiere), Dinar Dirham (Platinum), Wanxiang Blockchain Labs (Platinum), Santander (Gold), ConsenSys (Gold), Ether.Camp (Gold) and Synereo (Gold).

Subsequently, she introduced prominent research and development members of Ethereum. These were, in the order they spoke, Martin Becze, Péter Szilágyi, Dr. Christian Reitwiessner, Alex Van de Sande, Viktor Trón, and Vitalik Buterin.

Prior to technical presentations, Peter Van Valkenburgh talked about the regulatory considerations which the Ethereum Foundation and all associated developers had to adhere to. Ming Chan stressed the utmost importance of following the law depending on which jurisdiction they were in.

Topics discussed on the first day included:

- Vitalik Buterin spoke about Ethereum in twenty five minutes.

- Philip Daian spoke about smart contract research.

- Vlad Zamfir spoke about the Casper protocol.

Towards the end of the first day, Vitalik Buterin took to the stage for the second time to talk about the "Mauve Revolution". He showcased the advanced stage at which preparations for the transition from proof of work to proof of stake were taking place.

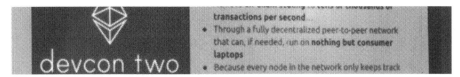

On the 20th September, the opening presentations focused on the subject of security. A panel discussion consisting of Martin Swende, Vitalik, Dr. Christian Reitwiessner, Raine Revere and Philip Daian took place. They discussed how they could improve the testing and development of smart contracts.

Later on during the day, discussion moved on to Ethereum development tools such as Embark and Truffle. They are both development frameworks that help to make development more productive by providing the necessary tools.

During the second day, Matthew Tan announced that Santander were vying to become to first bank to issue digital cash on the blockchain. Members of the audience were very ecstatic as soon as they heard the news.

After an introduction from Ming Chan, Marley Gray of Microsoft, the premiere sponsor of Devcon2, was the first to take the stage on the last day. He was proud to announce "Bletchley v1" (a tool which makes the creation of private based Ethereum blockchains easier). Other presentations on the final day (dubbed Demo day) included announcements and demonstrations of approximately thirty different innovative and inspiring projects. Unfortunately, not all one hundred pledged presentations could pitch their projects. Some of the most interesting talks were:

- Vlad Zemfir gave updates on sharding. Its objective is to provide unlimited scalability of the network.

- Heiko Hees demonstrated the Raiden Network, Ethereum's new lightning network.

- Zooko Wilcox presented Zcash. It could help add privacy to Ethereum.

- Julian Zawistowski introduced the Golem project.

- Rouven Heck and Dr. Christian Lundkvist spoke about uPort. It is a self-sovereign identity and key management system.

During the last hour, a panel consisting of individuals including Matthew Spoke, Marley Gray and Victor Wong discussed Ethereum usage in the enterprise environment. Privacy, scalability and security were covered. Matthew Spoke wrapped up the day with his presentation titled "The Future of Digital Infrastructure" at 17:15 Shanghai Time.

Ethereum developers applauded the audience as the highly eventful three day conference in Shanghai, China ended. They valued the Ethereum community.

Since the 18th September, the Ethereum network had been under constant attack from an unknown entity. It was causing significant delays (2-3x reduction in the rate at which blocks created) in transaction times. It was described as a denial of service (DoS) attack. Vitalik Buterin suggested two hard forks. The first one of these would address the urgent network health issues. There were a negligible number people against it (no one wanted to stay on DoS vulnerable blockchain).

On the 29th September, the ICONOMI ICO crowdsale ended at 19:59:59 UTC. It had raised $10,682,516.42. Simply put, it is a digital assets management platform that enables simple access to a variety of digital assets. It is being developed in Slovenia by Cashila.

On the 13th October, the third hard fork called "Tangerine Whistle" was announced after some delay due to developers testing it thoroughly. It's objective was to successfully stop the DoS attacks. Five days later, the hard fork kicked in:

Block #2,463,000 (Reward 5 ETH) October 18th 2016 at 01:19:31 PM UTC

On the 11th November, the Golem crowdsale began and ended. It hit its goal in a mere 29 minutes. It raised a total of $8,600,000 (which was the target ceiling). It is described as a "decentralised sharing economy of computing power" which enables users who participate to make money by renting out their processing power.

On the 15th November, the fourth hard fork of the Ethereum network protocol, Spurious Dragon, was announced with the corresponding block number. Its aim was to erase empty accounts that the unknown attacker/s used to bloat the Ethereum blockchain. After numerous tests of the code, the developers eventually released the mandatory updates which kicked in on the following Tuesday:

Block #2,675,000 (Reward 5 ETH) November 22nd 2016 at 04:15:44 PM UTC

During and after the period of technical difficulties, the US$ value of one Ether had descended to a nine month low on the 6th December. At the time of publication of this book, these lows have not been broken. What follows are the volatile US$ values of one unit of Ether account on the top five volume exchanges

	Price	Low	Open	Close	High	Volume
Bitfinex	7.20	5.86	6.68	7.71	7.88	173,583.38
Kraken	7.24	5.92	6.71	7.77	7.90	153,285.28
BTC-e	7.14	5.87	6.67	7.61	7.90	141,245.51
Poloniex	7.19	5.85	6.69	7.69	7.87	77,702.81
GDAX	6.75	6.41	6.69	6.81	7.11	47,706.85

Due to conversion rates between ETH/BTC and BTC/USD (averages across array of exchanges, there are many estimates of how low the Ether value went. However, the 6th December was the day on which the low was attained. Poloniex continued to dominate the ETH/BTC exchange rate in terms of volume (over 50%).

At the end of 2016, the market capitalisation of Ethereum had reached roughly US$697,000,000. It has risen approximately ten fold since the beginning of the year. Also, it was clear that the network had become more resilient to attacks as Vitalik Buterin wanted greater focus on Metropolis (the next stage of the project).

Other events which occurred during this period were:

- On the 26th September, the crowdsale of a decentralised eSports application called First Blood finished. A total of US$6,267,767 was raised. It took only a few minutes to surpass the US$5,500,000 target. The native token is 1ST.

- On the 13th October, a Ukraine-based called Liqui added Ether trading.

- On the 30th November, an exchange called Bitsane were happy to announce that they had initiated the trading pairs ETH/BTC, ETH/USD and ETH/EUR.

- On the 2nd December, an exchange called BTC Alpha added Ether.

- On the 16th December, somebody gain unauthorised access to the database of the official Ethereum forum at http://forum.ethereum.org

I. BLOCK NUMBER 3,000,000 SUCCESSFULLY TIMESTAMPED

II. PROGRESS TOWARDS METROPOLIS

III. ENTERPRISE ETHEREUM ALLIANCE (EEA) LAUNCHED

IV. ÐΞVCON3 ANNOUNCED TO TAKE PLACE IN CANCUN, MEXICO

V. MARKET CAPITALISATION OF ETHEREUM SURGED

11

ENTERPRISE INTEREST AND MARKET CAPITALISATION SURGE

"You are not going to get people to leave Facebook by explaining to them that they should not use it. It is so convenient and they will stick with what is convenient. It has to be about ease of use. I think there will be services that are just better. Things we can not do right now. People will end up using Ethereum without knowing it." - Dr. Aron Fischer

Details had begun to emerge about a secretive project aiming to make the utilisation of Ethereum more appealing to mainstream corporate firms including Microsoft, Intel and UBS. It would become known as the Enterprise Ethereum Alliance. Blockchain technology generally had become one of the top topics of IT enterprise entering 2017. There was strong belief that, as Ethereum continued to grow and simultaneously attract interest from businesses across the globe, it would become the most commonly used blockchain technology available.

Ethereum was, going into 2017, a blockchain valued at just shy of US1 billion according to its market capitalisation. An array of software was readily available for developers of many hues and colours. Research on proof of stake (Casper), Swarm, Whisper and a light client were still in progress. Collaboration between the Ethereum Foundation and the corporate business world was well underway.

On New Year's Day 2017, in terms of market capitalisation, Ethereum still remained second to Bitcoin. According to www.coinmarketcap.com, the approximate market capitalisations of some of the top cryptocurrencies on this day were:

	Market Capitalisation	Value of One Unit of Account
Bitcoin, BTC	~US$16,056,777,863	~US$998.73
Ethereum, ETH	~US$720,735,075	~US$8.24
Ripple, XRP	~US$237,825,076	~US$0.006545
Litecoin, LTC	~US$220,080,457	~US$4.48
Monero, XMR	~US$187,365,475	~US$13.71
Ethereum Classic, ETC	~US$120,637,927	~US$1.38
Dash, DASH	~US$78,018,285	~US$11.16
NEM, XEM	~US$30,907,529	~US$0.003434
Dogecoin, DOGE	~US$24,157,291	~US$0.000225
Zcash, ZEC	~US$17,079,870	~US$48.89

On the 19th January, it was reported that members of the Ethereum and Zcash development teams had begun to collaborate on research addressing privacy in blockchains. New code had been tested using the Solidity programming language.

Four days prior to this, a milestone block number was timestamped:

Block #3,000,000 (Reward 5 ETH) January 15th 2017 at 10:10:35 AM UTC

On the 14th February, Vitalik Buterin posted an official Ethereum blog article in which he updated the community on progress and the next scheduled software release called Metropolis. However, there was no concrete time set for when it would be released. Features likely to be included in Metropolis were outlined. Vitalik Buterin was quoted as saying:

"During the last month and a half, the Ethereum Core development and research teams have been building upon the progress made in the last year, and with the specter of last year's security issues now well behind us, work has [begun] full force on implementing the Metropolis hard fork."

On the 28th February, a group of global companies from industries such as finance, software, insurance etc. formed the "Enterprise Ethereum Alliance". It was formally revealed at an event in Brooklyn, NY, USA. On the official website at http://entethalliance.org, the following describes the mission of this group:

"The Enterprise Ethereum Alliance connects Fortune 500 enterprises, startups, academics, and technology vendors with Ethereum subject matter experts. Together, we will learn from and build upon the only smart contract supporting blockchain currently running in real-world production – Ethereum – to define enterprise-grade software capable of handling the most complex, highly demanding applications at the speed of business."

Via a televised speech, Vitalik Buterin called for collaboration between corporations planning to develop blockchain applications on Ethereum. It would help join private blockchains in the corporate world to the larger public Ethereum network. This, in turn, would increase the adoption of Ethereum. What follows is a list of the ten most popular "Launch Members" of the Enterprise Ethereum Alliance:

Accenture PLC	—a management consulting and professional services company
BP	—a British multinational oil and gas company
Credit Suisse	—a Swiss multinational financial services holding company
ING	—a Dutch multinational banking and financial services corporation
Intel	—an American multinational corporation and technology company
J.P.Morgan	—U.S. multinational banking and financial services holding company
Microsoft	—an American multinational technology company
Thomson Reuters	—a multinational mass media and information firm
Santander	—a Spanish banking group centred on Banco Santander, S.A.
UBS	—a Swiss global financial services company

Other companies part of the EEA include BBVA, BlockApps, Brainbot, BNY Mellon, CME Group, ConsenSys, Chronicled, Cryptape, Fubon Financial, IC3, The Institutes, Monax Industries, Nuco, String, Telindus, Tendermint, VidRoll and Wipro.

At the launch event, some representatives said they chose Ethereum due to it being a heavily tested, resilient and trusted platform. They wanted to see enhancements the privacy, security and scalability of the Ethereum blockchain, making it better suited to business applications. Launch members hoped that it would help them streamline some of their processes.

On the 2nd March, a social trading network called eToro announced that they had made it possible for its users to trade Ether. Yoni Assia, co-founder and the CEO of eToro, was quoted as saying:

> *"With a market cap of over 1B USD we see more and more interest from our traders world wide to trade and invest in Ethereum."*

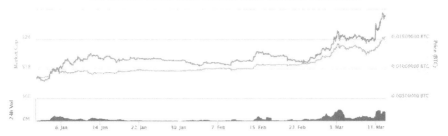

On the 12th March, the market capitalisation of Ethereum surpassed US$2 billion for the first time (see chart above). Ethereum had attained a cap more than 10% of Bitcoin's market cap. The value of its native cryptocurrency, Ether, had increased roughly 50% over the past three days. According to www.cryptocompare.com, the US$ prices per unit of Ether account on this day were the following:

	Price	Low	Open	Close	High	Volume
GDAX	22.52	21.33	21.64	23.39	24.25	263,530.04
Bitfinex	22.25	21.05	21.30	23.20	23.23	224,815.24
Kraken	22.30	21.00	21.29	23.30	23.40	122,099.18
BTC-e	22.07	21.00	21.15	22.99	22.99	88,899.02
Poloniex	22.28	21.11	21.31	23.24	23.31	79,233.02

Also, the top five ETH/BTC markets in terms of Ether volume on the same day were:

	Price	Low	Open	Close	High	Volume
Poloniex	0.01859	0.01784	0.01815	0.01902	0.01949	856,642.61
Kraken	0.01859	0.01773	0.01819	0.01898	0.01940	200,782.89
Bitinfex	0.01857	0.01789	0.01815	0.01898	0.01949	99,924.19
HitBTC	0.01859	0.01797	0.01818	0.01899	0.01962	92,827.50
BTC-e	0.01857	0.01785	0.01811	0.01902	0.01935	59,918.32

On the 15th March, details were unveiled of the next Ethereum Developers Conference. ÐΞVCON3 will occur on the 1st-4th November 2017 in Cancun, Mexico. Based on the popularity and reception received at the previous two events in London and Shanghai, it is likely to be a sellout event. An official website at https://ethereumfoundation.org/devcon3/ had already gone live.

Since the market capitalisation surpassed US$2 billion, it continued to break all time highs over the following few days. On the 16th March, it had more than doubled to over US$4 billion. Ether trading volume (24h) over all known and recognised exchanges had also superseded, for a few hours, that of Bitcoin at approximately US$450 million. The following table shows the increase of the US$ values of both the market capitalisation of Ethereum and one unit of Ether account:

Date	Market Capitalisation	Value of 1 ETH
12th February 2016	~US$384,000,000	~US$5.00
1st January 2017	~US$740,000,000	~US$8.30
12th March 2017	~US$2,000,000,000	~US$22.30
16th March 2017	~US$4,000,000,000	~US$44.80
17th March 2017	~US$4,915,000,000	~US$54.70

It would remain to be seen whether or not Ethereum could sustain the momentum it had gained over the past few months as the result of institutional investor interest. One unit of Ether account had exceeded US$50, the developer community were busy preparing for Metropolis and hundreds of decentralised applications were being worked on. A promising, innovative and inspiring future lay ahead.

Made in the USA
Coppell, TX
23 June 2021